Poetry Ireland Review 65

Edited by **Biddy Jenkinson**

© Copyright Poetry Ireland Ltd. 2000

Poetry Ireland Ltd./Éigse Éireann Teo. gratefully acknowledges the assistance of The Arts Council/An Chomhairle Ealaíon, the Arts Council of Northern Ireland and FÁS.

Patrons of Poetry Ireland/Éigse Éireann

Grogan's Castle Lounge
Dr. G. Rosenstock
Eastern Washington University
Fearon, O'Neill, Rooney
Daig Quinn
Twomey Steo Ltd.
Kevin Connolly
Neville Keery

Desmond Windle
Joan & Joe McBreen
Dillon Murphy & Co.
Office Of Public Works
Richard Murphy
Occidental Tourist Ltd.
Winding Stair Bookshop

Poetry Ireland warmly invites individuals, cultural groups and commercial organisations to become Patrons. Patrons are entitled to reclaim tax at their highest rate for all donations of between £101.00 and £10,000. For more details please contact the Director, at Bermingham Tower, Dublin Castle, Dublin 2, Ireland or phone 01. 6714632 or e-mail: poetry@iol.ie.

Poetry Ireland Review is published quarterly by Poetry Ireland Ltd. The Editor enjoys complete autonomy in the choice of material published. The contents of this publication should not be taken to reflect either the views or the policy of the publishers.

ISSN: 0332-2998
ISBN: 1-902121-03-1

Editorial Assistant: Anna Boner
Typesetting: Anna Boner
Cover Design: Colm Ó Cannain
Typography: Barry Hannigan
Cover Photographs: Mark Granier

Printed in Ireland by ColourBooks Ltd., Baldoyle Industrial Estate, Dublin 13.

Contents   Poetry Ireland Review 65

	3	Editorial
Sheila O'Hagan	5	September the Fourth
Paddy Bushe	7	Freagra Scéine ar Aimheirgin
Paddy Bushe	9	Final Version
Tom McFadden	10	Watering the Sunshine
Dawn Sullivan	11	Nesting Mouse
Dawn Sullivan	12	Lissadell 1996
Dawn Sullivan	14	**Extract from The Muse...**
Dennis O'Driscoll	16	**Pickings and Choosings**
Kevin Kiely	18	Hymn to Aphrodite
Liz McSkeane	19	Last Night, You Offered Me a Glass
Nuala Ní Chonchúir	20	The White Mantle
Eileen Casey	21	The Captive Muse
Eamonn Lynskey	22	The Fugitive Muse
Tony Curtis	24	Nude
Moyra Donaldson	26	The Glimmering Girl
Gary Allen	27	The Broiler House
Rita Kelly	28	Eavan Boland in Carlow
Eva Bourke	**30**	**The Dragon Slayer**
Eva Bourke	35	In Duiche Iar
Eva Bourke	*37*	Travels with Gandolpho
Deirdre Brennan	39	June
Deirdre Brennan	40	The Last Observance
D. Nurkse	42	The Stray
John Knowles	43	The Fulcrum
Jean O'Brien	44	The Angels
Merryn Williams	45	Charlotte's Baby
Mary Wickham	46	Foot
Patrick Moran	47	Birthplace
Patrick Moran	48	Faith Healer in Age
Howard Wright	50	Warm Milk
Pádraig Ó'Snodaigh	*51*	**The Handsomest Man in Ireland**
Paul Perry	54	Sundays
Paul Perry	56	Blessed is the Fruit
Greg Delanty	58	The Scalding
Louis de Paor	61	Focaldeoch
Harry Clifton	64	Red Fox Country
Peter Sirr	66	The Hunt
	68	China
Colette Connor	70	Redemption
Denise Blake	71	Rathlin Island
Ronald Tamplin	72	To Drive a Wise Man Wild

Chris Agee	74	Requiem
Patricia Burke Brogan	75	The Painting
Bernard O'Donoghue	76	Two Fiddlers at Scully's
Maurice Harmon	77	Frozen Phoenix
Maurice Harmon	78	Shunkan
Derry O'Sullivan	79	Cogito Ergo Sum
Pádraig Mac Fhearghusa	80	Allagar
Bríd Ní Mhóráin	81	I bhFothair na Manach
Una O'Higgins O'Malley	82	Just God
Art Murphy	83	Here and Now
Fiona Brennan	84	Feeding the Muse
Manny Blacksher	85	The Guillotine
Cecilia McGovern	86	The 'Coothrements'
Máire de Búrca	87	**Om Namaha Shivaya**
Fred Johnston	93	What Heroes Are For
Tom French	94	Night Drive
Lynne Wycherley	96	Watching the Tide on Inch Strand
Padraig Rooney	97	The Nuns at Poll an tSnámh
Seán Lysaght	98	A Stone's Throw
Gerard Donovan	99	Steps to Possession
Tom McIntyre	100	Menage-à-Trois-na-Maidne
Rita Ann Higgins	101	They Never Wear Coats
Rita Ann Higgins	103	Our Brother the Pope
John McAuliffe	105	After Goethe's Fifth Roman Elegy
Gerry Murphy	106	Ode to Catullus
Kate Dempsey	107	Running Out
Michael Cronin	108	**Cheating Death**
Stuart Lane	111	Ancient Earthworks
Patrick Gerard Burke	111	Break Time
Jessica Ní Chuaig	111	Imprints
Bob Slaymaker	111	Disclaimer
Mark Granier	111	Approaching Dun Aengus
Iggy McGovern	112	Museless
Anatoly Kudryavitsky	112	Poet and Poverty
Gabriel Rosenstock	113	Broighill sna Dugaí
Adam Rudden	113	Bury the Coffins
Clair Dillon	113	If Sympathy is. . .
Margaret Toppin	113	In My Veggie Box
John O'Donnell	114	Where a Poem Comes From
John Enfield	115	After the Workshop
Christine Broe	116	No Poem
Dennis O'Driscoll	117	**Enveloped in Poetry**
	119	Notes on Contributors
	124	Books Received

Editorial

To submit a poem to a magazine is like putting out a tender plant in the spring. I'd hate to be anybody's late May frost, so please let me explain the mathematics of the selection. The sums are horribly simple. 1,605 poems came in for this edition (between November and March), 1,545 of them must be sent home.

The selection is made by an editor who suffers, as editors do, from prejudices and from the tendency to overcorrect them, from blind spots, enthusiasms, bad days and allergies. After repeated readings the 1,600 were reduced to 200 poems that have become familiar and dear to this reader. Only 70 of these can be accomodated.

In the final selection there is a large element of chance. Some poems seem to link together. Others are needed for contrast and variety. A beginner wtih a good poem should get a chance but this can mean leaving out an established author. In short, non inclusion says nothing about the merit of the poem.

I have squeezed in as many poems as possible and I have tried to select a variety of styles. Few poems in fixed form were submitted. Not a single dán díreach came in, few sonnets, neither ballad nor amhrán. Perhaps some readers might like to experiment with traditional forms and send me the poems in time for our next edition?

Niamh Morris who has been managing editor of the Review for the last nine years has left. All the writers who have experienced her friendly encouragement and the editors who have benefited from her expertise will regret her departure, while rejoicing that new opportunities are presenting themselves to her. Go n-eirí go geal léi sa phost nua.

Mo bhuíochas leo siúd a sheol dánta and aistí chugainn. Tá súil agam go mbainfidh sibh go léir taithneamh as eagrán seo an tSamhraidh, tiomnaithe do Bhé na filíochta, pé in Éirinn í.

— Biddy Jenkinson
April 2000.

Sheila O'Hagan

September the fourth

At four am today my lover died.
He didn't reach for me or call my name,
Dreaming he would waken by my side,
But turned his face and shuddered as some shame
Or haunting shook him and his mouth gave cry
To a portentous and unearthly pain.

Between darkness and dawn that cry of pain
And nothing warm has touched me since it died.
Some ethos of cold starlight I can't name
Possessed my love while he lay by my side,
Something strange, unhuman, born of shame.
He had not said goodbye, called out or cried.

Some ghost or spirit left his mouth that cried
Out and he'd gone from me, had gone in pain
Into an alien world, yet as he died
He drew my spirit to him, gave her my name.
Something possessed him as he left my side.
His face was turned away as though in shame.

I took his absent face and murmured shame
To that which claimed him, for my love had cried
As though some shady trafficking in pain,
Some curse or Judas-kiss by which he died
Unknowingly in another's name,
Had come to term as he lay down beside

The one he loved. Perhaps lying by his side,
Fearful in sleep, I had called up that shame
And he, my love, unknowingly had cried
Out in redemption for another's pain,
As though a chosen victim. My love died
Because some cursèd spirit took his name.

For he was loved and honoured in his name
And I, as I lay sleeping by his side
Guarding his innocence, knew of no shame.
On the stark cusp of dark and dawn he cried
Aloud so strange my heart burned cold with pain.
Not one warm thought has touched me since he died.

Still I call his name. All hope has died.
My unspent love's my pain. I have not cried.
Such is winter's shame, all's bare outside.

This poem won the inaugural Strokestown
International Poetry Competition, 2000.

Paddy Bushe

Freagra Scéine ar Aimheirgin

Más tusa gaoth na mara
    Is mise an fharraige om shearradh féin faoid leoithne
Más tonn díleann thú
    Is sliogán folamh mé ag tnúth led theacht
Más tú gáir na stoirme
    Is mé lapadaíl na taoide i mbrothall nóna
Más damh seacht mbeann thú
    Tiocfad suas go mánla chugat ar aiteann
Más seabhac thú ar an bhfaill
    Beannód thú le liricí fuiseogacha
Más deor drúchta faoin ngréin thú
    Brúfad féar na maidne go bog leat
Más tú is áille a fhásann
    Bláthód leat bliain ar bhliain
Más torc ar mire thú
    Cuirfead geasa gáire ar na fiacla fada agat
Más bradán thú sa linn
    Meallfad cuileoga ina gcéadta chugat
Más loch ar mhá thú
    Raghad go tóin poill ionat
Más tú rún na héigse
    Mise na naoi mBéithe agat
Má bhíonn faobhar ort chun troda
    Cuirfead ceangal na ceanúlachta ort
Má bhíonn tinfeadh á adhaint sa cheann agat
    Séidfead síol na tine duit

Tá fhios ag mo chroí istigh cé réitigh an bealach dom,
Cé ba réalt eolais, cé bhronn grian agus gealach orm,
Agus in ainneoin na gcloch seo, is an solas ag dul in éag,
Bead-sa scáth ar scáth leat, focal ar fhocal leis an ngaoth.

Paddy Bushe

Scéine's Reply to Aimherigin

If you are the wind on the sea/ I am the water tingling under the breeze/ If you are a wave in a flood/ I am an empty shell dreaming of your coming/ If you are the roar of a storm/ I am the tide lapping in the noon heat/ If you are the stag of seven horns/ I will pick my way to you gracefully through furze/ If you are a hawk on the cliff/ I will bless you with lyrics of larksong/ If you are a dewdrop in the sun/ I will gently bruise the morning grass with you/ If you are the fairest of flowers/ I will blossom year upon year with you/ If you are a maddened boar/ I will charm your tusks into laugher/ If you are a salmon in the pool/ I will lure infinities of insects to you/ If you a lake in the plain/ I will plumb your very depths/ If you are the essence of poetry/ I am all of your muses/ If you are edging towards a fight/ I will bewitch you to bluntness/ If you are kindling an inspiration in the mind/ I will blow on the seed of the fire for you/ I know in my heart who made the way smooth for me,/ Was star of knowledge to me, gave the sun and moon to me,/ And though the stones close in, and light moves towards its end,/ We will live in our shadow, word for word with the wind.

Aimheirgin Glúngheal, one of the sons of Milesius, was the poet, seer and lawmaker of the fist Celtic invaders, according to *Leabhar Gabhála,* or *Book of Invasion*s. His wife, Scéine, died shortly before they reached Ireland. According to legend, she is buried beneath a stone alignment near Waterville, Co. Kerry. The stones are aligned on the setting sun on Midwinter's Day. Amheirgin is said to have composed the poem beginning 'I am the wind on the sea' when he set foot on land just below the stone alignment.
21 Nollaig 1999

Paddy Bushe

Final Version

i.m. Michael Hartnett

Too early. Yes, all of that. But now you've said
A farewell to all language, and are translated
To a version where, definitively yourself,
Sharing elements with hares and otters,
And raising pewter mugs with spailpín poets,
You can hear the pulse-music you knew well
Lies beyond all poems, and before them,
And cannot be lost in the translation.

Tom McFadden

Watering the Sunshine

Time in its ninth decade had diminished the light,
leaving so little to illuminate her hallways of the mind.
Thought had to probe its way through the passages now,
wondering, in the dimness, which way to turn.
To reacquaint her with achievement,
the fragile figure had been led to the front of the summer yard,
where the fresh angle of morning still invited a shadow line —
that old day-new day realm of grass dichotomized:
half dimmed in last coating of night,
half bright.

'Water aimed toward the sun will hopelessly evaporate;
water only into the shadow.'
The words dripped, one by one,
into the remains of cognitive fertility,
while her grip slowly closed
around the nozzle gently nudged into her hand,
followed by exit of footsteps.

Alone, she stood on the shadow line,
while the words continued to drip in echoes,
aspiring to soak more profoundly toward the roots;
but, the passageways were so dim,
and, in such dearth of light,
it proved so very hard for the flowing to choose its way.
Wrinkles tightened above the remains of light
in mighty struggle to perceive the itinerary between day and night.

When at last those wrinkles fell into their unfolding,
the frail figure slowly manifested its route of decision
by shuffling one full turn upon the shadow line.
Balanced between the halves of time,
the instructed shadow-gardener slowly raised her nozzle,
then squeezed.
With drops of water landing onto her old-fashioned shoes,
edging the shadow that stretched behind her,
she assumed a good stance inside her own darkness . . .
then carefully watered the sunshine.

Dawn Sullivan

Nesting Mouse

The day I moved a spade,
to plant a Christmas-flowering clematis
I disturbed a log from the wood pile
and damaged a brown-backed, buff-bellied wood-mouse
in my garden, nesting away winter

It seemed alright
Then I crouched close to mouse-level
saw its sides going like a dolls' house bellows
barely above the sound of crickets, that miniature scream

When I did with my spade — the kindest thing . . .
it fell back — with only a trickle from its whiskers
like the Tailor of Gloucester's scarlet twist
and its dolls' house hands — almost humanly pleading

After their Scanner has spoken
the Perfect Ones infer
that I should not demand to increase
the pile of seconds in this sale we call Life

Politely, those Perfect Ones infer
and so respectfully — how wouldn't it be —
the Kindest Thing. . . ?

I am thinking of it. . .
while you are still easily melted
as the invisible star in a snow crystal
Less audible than a word
of mouth or machine?

Dawn Sullivan

Lissadell: 1996

'The light of evening Lissadell
Great windows open to the south'
— W.B. Yeats

From Rosses Point by the shimmer
of lilac and silver and rose
with autumn to Lissadell,
footstepping poetry:
finding the shock —
of great windows no longer open to the south;
mostly shuttered or boarded
Declaring their redundance to the sea

A care-takers solitary light bulb?
Huddle of geranium pots, humble on the back steps
Elsewhere enough light left, in the darkening air
for glimpsing through glass shadowed things:
shape of kettle —

. . . And the Bear!
A world ago in Holy Russia shot:
moth-balding now, child-broken paw missing,
glue-grizzled snarl frozen
fabulously more. . .
Because the winter of the Tsars has gone.

This house breathes stronger in neglect
than any scrubbed by the National Trust;
Here by twilight we can tell
even before the flaking and the rust,
They did not build Lissadell to be beautiful

But granite and square;
as Constance said:
'. . . a Barracks against the Natives!'
that ancient dread, beyond the imperial shrubbery

Entrance porch
empty of any plaque
about her part in a nation's striving, to recover
its own muffled pulse of heart
Neutral terse notice:
'. . . Home of the Gore-Booths and
childhood home of Constance Markiewicz.'

For such a family's metallic gravitas
what could be worse than a daughter —
embracing Treason and firing squad at dawn?
Saved for life-sentence:

'. . . solely on account of her sex.'

We've come from the National Museum:
from her anonymous guns under glass,
and disappointment
at her bronze drawing-room head; its spiritual absence
but noting, the essence of herself: C.M. — she signed aslant:
Yellow faded chain-stitch on a prison towel
initialled like a sampler; mocking
all leisured shooting of the grouse
— all Dresden destinies,
of clipped winged angels of the house!

It is the moment of turning around to make something last —
Straining to see — a child out late
with summer and rebellion against embroidery:
Roaming past us, some white frocked moth,
somewhere along this woody avenue of the unending past. . .
where only we pass less and ghostly

After Lissadel's signed exit, suddenly —
more powerful than autumn,
on the high-road, are words
returned to their nurturing-place

And we —
strange shadows, another moment rooted
re-read that Poem
framed upon the tree.

Dawn Sullivan

Extract from 'The Muse: Symbol for Civilisation'

Throughout all our millenia of survival, we have *only* survived philosophically by symbols. Reductive, industrial rationalism encourages psychic chaos. Symbolic thinking enables us to constructively embrace unescapable paradoxes. A symbol is loaded with opposite depths of meaning that it alone has power to unite, so our responses to it remain those of psychic growth.

We need the Muse now, more than ever before, as an inspirational symbol of restoring (in all fields) symbolic thought. That Greek idea of the Muse and all her sister-selves as daughters of Mnemosyne, Goddess of Memory, is now crucial. Because this new century has put us: ". . . in danger of losing our minds. . ."

Professor Susan Greenfield has voiced this broadly felt anxiety about the way the intelligence of memory is being corroded by so many mechanistic processes. We are the first generation of the perpetual present; what might be coined "news on the hour" mileu of instant gratification.

Oceans of mass-produced, automated visual stimuli refuse us the inner eye of reflection. The speed of new communication can be antagonistic to creativity in ideas and relationships.

Creativity is the energy of transformation. Transformations need time. Time and technology are enemies. . . Not for nothing did the sexual union of Zeus and Mnemosyne, Goddess of Memory, last nine days and nights to produce the Muses. Such prolonged coupling with Memory is a metaphor for a sanctury of time-space that we all need to effect any positive transformation. The Muse, as a protective symbol of the time-space to think holistically, could benefit all arts and sciences. Being so multi-dimensional, she will not only defend us from excesses and obsessions of tunnel vision, but flex our imaginative reflexes to the utmost. She could wake up our language to make contact with the frigid jargon of the laboratory that speaks the future. Because of her origins, she could restore us to friendship with the earth.

In *The White Goddess*, Graves' literary monument to her, he emphasised her ability to drive men mad. I see her as a last hope for our mental health.

There is a healing energy about the verb she has generated: "to muse", its meaning: "to ponder", "to meditate". Musing has nothing to do with any intellectual sausage-machine of unquestioningly reprocessing received wisdoms. A "museum" may now be reduced to a repository of cultural artefacts, but it could become again a word for what society most needs: a public meeting place to shape our future through philosophical debate. In ancient Greece "museum" became another word for school. Now education is robotically shackled to industry and slave of the economy, the Muse reminds us it should be about spiritual enrichment. Her verb is not only then a gift to poets. "To muse" implies what we will always most need; time and freedom to enquire and dream. . .

Dennis O'Driscoll

Pickings and Choosings

'Poetry is a bodily activity with a high voltage of muse energy.'
— Seamus Heaney, *The Times*, 27 March 1999

'A poem is as clear as a drink of water, as rigorous (and as rare) as an honest judge, as packed full of meaning as a ripe apple is packed with white flesh.'
— Theo Dorgan, *The Irish Times*, 22 May 1999

'The thing that nourishes poetry is not an ocean; it's a very small mountain stream.'
— Derek Walcott, *BBC Radio 3*, April 1999

'Poetry is religious in its contemplation of experience under the eye of eternity. It helps us to live our lives in the face of destruction. It can give us a spiritual strength.'
— Seamus Heaney, *The Sunday Times*, 30 January 2000

'The problem of being a poet/ Is the problem of being always right.'
— Paul Durcan, *Greetings to Our Friends in Brazil*, 1999

'The literal-minded should be kept from poems.'
— P.J. Kavanagh, *The Times Literary Supplement*, 6 August 1999

'Poets who confuse art and life often make a mess of both.'
— Christian Wiman, *Poetry*, January 1999

'It is not necessarily bad news that more people write poems than read them: it suggests that the urge to create is itchier than the urge to consume.'
— Robert Winder, *Independent on Sunday*, 21 March 1999

'Poetry by its very nature resists the spiritual devastation induced by the mass media.'
—Czeslaw Milosz, *Partisan Review*, Winter 1999

'Love is the charge behind the lyric, technical mastery its muscle.'
— John Montague, *Fortnight,* February 1999

'Poetry is language articulating itself at its most acute. To quicken language to that pitch of arousal you have to be in bed with the Muse of that language.'
— Cathal Ó Searcaigh, *H.U.,* Winter 1999/ 2000

'Love poetry is not dead, it is in a state of arousal.'
— Craig Raine, *The Guardian,* 13 February 1999

'Writing a poem is a sexual act'.
— Ruth Valentine, *Poetry London,* Summer 1999

'I write poems because I have to. It's like sex. You are attracted to your beloved for reaons that are neither rational nor entirely conscious.'
— Dana Gioia, *Forbes Magazine,* 17 May 1999

'To say death is regrettable is only saying something about death, but to communicate that feeling is saying something about life'.
— Bernard O'Donoghue, *Oxford Poetry,* Summer 1999

'I had two children. . . It is the greatest act of creativity and the one which is most likely to make you question other forms of creativity.'
— Eavan Boland, *Irish Tatler,* 1999

'If any of you are poets and want to write poems about your children, for heaven's sake don't publish them until they've left school.'
— Michael Yeats, *RTE Radio 1,* March 1999

'My unborn son became one of my muses. . .'
— Penelope Shuttle, *PBS Bulletin,* Winter 1999

'If the poem has no obvious destination, there's a chance that we'll be all setting off on an interesting ride.'
— Paul Muldoon, *Harper's,* September 1999

'Trains are the best places to write. There is something about the rhythm of a train that helps you to write, especially poetry.'
— Ian McMillan, *The Times,* 15 July 1999

Kevin Kiely

Hymn to Aphrodite
from 'Plainchant for a Sundering'

The seaweed in your golden arch is another delicacy
those pillars and spheres, the bowl of womanhood
its socketless eye a lone star

Far off the grapes mounted in the little moons

Give me seafood at will
that I can live off the lap of luxury, explore the
sunlit cave where wave upon wave presses your
wine down the halls of my ears

I walk barefoot and climb your neck with my tongue
and come up again and again to behold the eyes
half-open inward gazing

Then your back is a meadow stretching towards trees
your arms come down at dawn in clouds with fingers
of rain coiling

Take me in once more where evening and morning
are lost forever and time stops
the world dissolves into the magic
at the glimpsed heart of things
and the earth is swallowed in the rings of Saturn

Let it all go or end but no more the lost way
the way down the insane streets

Let it all come back to your kisses
in the present and future
and great pain and unspeakable loss find an answer

Liz Mc Skeane

Last Night, You Offered Me a Glass

Last night, you offered me a glass
and when I reached for it you smiled
and clasped my hand and held it close
and I smiled too. Then something changed,
you were not exactly you, not
the person you were meant to be —
a phantom lover, someone
I half-knew, more perfect, maybe,
touched me. I'm out of sorts all day,
sated with dream-love, my skin
alive with absence, memories
of us the way we'd never been.

Nuala Ní Chonchúir

The White Mantle

I am Caer, and
when the harvest is over
I seasonally adjust,
slipping through the gap
between this and the otherworld,
where I wear a white mantle
and I rush and slide
on Loch Béal Dragan.

I hiss and glide,
taking comfort in the
throb and thrum of wings
as I fly over Crotta Cliach.
In the hush of the reeds
I slip waist high, then neck deep
into the cooling water, forgetting
my flesh is still feathered.

I invade Aengus' sleep, caressing
his mind — willing him to need
me on waking — I take him
between my thighs and enjoy
the sway of my plump breasts.
He comes, and finds me among
my silver-chained sisters, the only
swan wearing links of gold.

Entwined together, feathers
and arms are made one,
and a shape-changed Aengus
flies three times around the lake
by my side, until we leave for
Brú na Bóinne where our songs
lull the people to sleep, and
my Mac Óg lives only for me.

I am Caer, and I have
discarded my white mantle.

Eileen Casey

The Captive Muse

That wily bird fills winter skies
fit to burst with swans.
A line, opening perhaps
to some quiet epiphany, brighter
than anything hung-out to dry,
feathers between the washing-up, that mad
dash to school and supermarket,
stroking up surer possibilities
in the choosing of a roast or stew.
A line,
quills its way around the rib of afternoon,
insisting in the hiss and steam
of squabbling children, to mate
pencil with the page.

By evening, as the light fans in,
it is barely whispered above rattling pots,
locking out as surely as a husband turns the key
to his domain — and later — stilled.
All trace of swan dissolved,
dinner plates returned upon the rack.

Eamonn Lynskey

The Fugitive Muse
For Tommy Halferty

You say it was the daily rape
drove you from my classroom. Stunned,
I watched you rouge your cheeks, put on
mascara, run your tongue on lipstick,

take a taxi into town. How
terrible those endless days
of searching out the places where
you'd most least likely be (you see

how well I know you, dear). At last,
the six-foot lesbian who holds
Fitzwilliam Square demurred at first,
then sold you back to me — So pale

and drawn and unforgiving. Better
far (you snarled) be whore dark wintry
nights near Leeson Bridge than fingered
for five years, then Publicly

Examined, poked and probed, pubic
juices oozing onto desk-tops,
a kind of fossilised graffiti. . .
See, my dear, my tears to see you

stand in lamplight at the kerb
determined to waylay each cruising
car — What quatrains have passed hands
across those lowered windows? For

that extra fiver will you offer
that so often you denied
to me? — That sudden burst of clear
translucent verse. . . No, no! Stay where

you are. We'll have another coffee
here in the Pembroke Bar. We'll
renegotiate our terms
of endearment, you and I —

I plead — I beg you will return.
I promise no more sacrifice
to inky adolescence — Tenderly,
I'll weigh each smallest hyphen

would best fit the narrow slit
between two syllables, then cover
you with careful kisses, love,
that you will stay with me forever.

Tony Curtis

Nude

She has been with me all winter.
I cannot say I hate her
for when I was young
I loved everything about her.
There were nights
I could have died for her.
Now there's an awful
pattern to our lives.

She arrives late September
carrying sacks of old books,
and pinned to her dress
or tied in her hair,
or buried in the folds
of her skin,
are those few new poems
I have waited all summer to hear.

But each year her price
goes a little higher
and I grow weary.
Night after night
she empties her grave.
Often she undresses
to the bone:
peeling her skin,
folding the wrinkled hide
over the bed
where she sups and stares.

Often she strips me too,
planting the tips
of her fingers
like roots in my eyes,
or pushing her tongue
deep into my mouth.

Bare. Naked. Nude —
unless you've ever
served her,
felt her cunning
on your lips,
you'll never know
the meaning of the word.

And yet,
one of these mornings
I'll find her
standing in the kitchen
dressed for the road,
coat, hat, scarf,
bags tied with string,
and I'll be on my knees
begging her to stay.

Moyra Donaldson

The Glimmering Girl

He's tying a Red Sedge
for those hot summer evenings
or those dead afternoons, July and August
when he can't quite decide
what to offer the occasional riser,
close under the bank.

she watches him beeswax the thread,
wind and tie, interweave fur and feather
until they become a living creature again

The body is hare's ear, spun on orange silk,
and ribbed with gold wire.
Wound all down the body from head to tail,
the hackle comes from a red cockerel.
The wings are Landrail, tied so as to lie
flat along the Sedge's back.
Finished, he holds it between his fingers,
lifts it into the light,
sees the graceful wheel of the line
as he lies it down soft as a snowflake

. . . beautiful as a red sedge
fluttering late in the evening sun
on a slow moving stream.
She rises — feels too late the hook,
the line tightening against her dash and desperation.

Gary Allen

The Broiler House

She is the fresh one
at the end of this line

of worn-out women with podgy faces
and brawny arms

hands viscid
with guts, giblets, membranes.

The heavy-set man behind them
in the blood flecked apron
is mouthing a dirty joke,

cleaver-raping moribund meat,
pink and gaping like an open mouth.

This is the beginning of seven children
and the loss of small things —

girlhood, innocence, church on Sunday,
the sanctity of flesh.

Rita Kelly

Eavan Boland in Carlow

So long ago, aeons out of mind,
way back in the mother of all the Muses:
Memory, when you came along the roads
not yet numbered as national routes
but named by the places they connected
together along a network of the familiar.

We met in a local hotel
the kind found in every town,
famous for its comfort, respectable,
well-known to the commercial traveller
long before he had become a company rep.
Full of mid-week crisis, quotas and commissions.
Arthur Miller kind of people not in turbid America
or in the Waldorf-Astoria, no, just a regular hotel
in the middle of the town
with company reps as isolated as intellectuals.
Dust motes and blue smoke funnelled
by the early spring sunshine above a carpet
which kept the mild hint of stale beer in its weave.

You came, always the generous mentor, to advise
to help and above all to reinforce the need
to keep the word as it was shaped.
To hold the line against the hard demands.
Not to give in.
Not to roll over and play dead
for questionable gain. To keep the line
as the line was made.

And then the Muse came up,
a thread of conversation.
Did I feel the intrusion
at the creative moment?
Did I hear the invocation
from the man who sat across the table

as he shaped and honed?
No, these high flown Greek goddesses
did not come between me and him.
There was no ghosting of inspiration,
I heard him breathe upon the stairs,
I saw him storm and pale from exhaustion.

But when you set your fancies free
perhaps they will come now to you
stepping through the cool of morning
across turbid America, Polyhymnia,
Thalia for the laugh and Terpsichore
light-footed and rhythmic to dance upon
the page.

These other women
these figments of male imaginings,
no, they never came between us.
Perhaps they visit women too,
women who care for rugby
kill for tickets to Landsdowne Road,
appraise themselves of the difference
between a dithyramb and a loose ruck,
show an interest in politics and play
the currency markets not just the commodities.

But we know our Zeus
that con-man, taking whatever shape or form it took
to have his way and penetrate
the everyday.
And to him a good lay is not just a lyrical poem
intended to be sung.

Eva Bourke

The Dragon Slayer

Beowulf: A New Translation, **Seamus Heaney** Faber & Faber, 1999. Price £14.99 (cased)

The Faber & Faber edition of *Beowulf* in a new translation by Seamus Heaney comes in a suitably sombre black dust jacket dripping with red. The world of the oldest Anglo-Saxon/Germanic epic, which was composed roughly between the 8th and 10th centuries, is dark, terror-filled and bloody: war, conquest, feuds and endless revenge are the order of the day, man-eating ogres and ogresses roam the wilderness; dragons, the most dangerous of all fiends, lie in wait in gloomy caves.

The poem is partly set in Denmark, where Beowulf twice helps the Danish king out of great difficulty, and for the last part in the land of the Geats in southern Sweden, Beowulf's own place of origin, and also of his end during his fight with the dragon. In style and content it is very close to the Germanic heroic epics collected in the younger Edda, it has the same heavy alliterative verse and four stress lines, the same plethora of kennings, all of which Wagner would carry to laughable extremes in his libretti for the opera cycle *Der Ring des Nibelungen.*

The minstrel's lay about Sigemund the dragon-slayer during the celebration of Beowulf's triumphant return to his homeland derives from this ancient mythological tradition, but because the author was probably an educated English monk who knew the scriptures and seems to have read Latin epics, the text shows these influences as well. In the hands of this poet-monk the story of a young hero eager to make his mark and incidentally rid a neighbouring country of a terrible marauder becomes a subtle, multi-layered and gripping narrative. The figure of the hero shines with a special light — he is compassionate, brave, proud and generous, loyal to his overlords and selflessly devoted to his young king. His reputation as a dangerous enemy and his royal wisdom hold the peace for fifty years in Geatland. This makes his death at the dragon's lair all the more catastrophic. The story ends on a terribly pessimistic note: the people are leaderless and without defence and face a certain future of raids and slaughter at the hands of their enemies.

I read *Beowulf* as a child, probably in prose form, and suffered nightly terrors with Grendelian faces pressing against my bedroom windows for some time after, and again as a teenager in an American high school as part of the senior curriculum where my early impression that *Beowulf* was comfortless and unredeemably bleak was reinforced. However, this may partly have been due to a singularly heavy-handed translation. All that is different now thanks to Seamus Heaney's brilliant adaptation.

Free of archaisms and appositions that hinder the flow of language, the contemporary, sometimes almost colloquial use of English allows the reader to sail along effortlessly. Compound nouns are only sprinkled through the text sparingly to give it just enough of that Old English flavour. There are some beauties though: the dragon for example is called vile sky-winger, sky-plague, sky-roamer, poison-breather, ground-burner. But most of the time Heaney says he just called a sword a sword. With enviable lightness of touch, while remaining true to the spirit and melody of the original text, he manages to make it recognisably his own. The narrator's tone is dignified and direct, but often also extravagant with the music of assonances and alliterations. For example, this is Beowulf talking of his victory over Grendel:

> He has done his worst but the wound will end him.
> He is hasped and hooped and hirpling with pain,
> limping and looped in it. Like a man outlawed
> for wickedness, he must await
> the mighty judgement of God in majesty.

'Hirpling' — which is not in my Concise Oxford — is a stroke of genius: delivered with unrestrained triumph, it takes the monster down many pegs to the ridiculous howling, gurgling half-thing he now is. Heaney says in his introduction, translating *Beowulf* into modern English was like taking a toy hammer to a megalith. But Herculean as the work may have been, it was clearly also a labour of love. There are delightfully tender moments as in the minstrel's account of the creation:

> . . . the clear song of a skilled poet
> telling with mastery of man's beginnings,
> how the Almighty had made the earth
> a gleaming plain girdled with waters,
> in His splendour He set the sun and the moon

> to be earth's lamplight. Lanterns for men,
> and filled the broad lap of the world
> with branches and leaves; and quickened life
> in every other thing that moved.

The language is marvellously concise; when Beowulf sets sail for Denmark for instance it almost sings the urgency and panache of the hero's journey across the sea:

> Men climbed eargerly up the gangplank
> sand churned in the surf, warriors loaded
> a cargo of weapons, shining war-gear in
> the vessel's hold, then heaved out,
> away with a will in their wood-wreathed ship.
> Over the waves, with the wind behind her
> and foam at her neck, she flew like a bird
> until her curved prow had covered the distance . . .

And at the end of the poem when Beowulf's funeral pyre has blazed, the hero, his helmets, shields and armour have been consumed by the flames and the people are mourning their lord, the lament of a woman reaches across the centuries to us with a terrible familiarity:

> A Geat woman too sang out in grief;
> with hair bound up, she unburdened herself
> of her worst fears, a wild litany
> of nightmare and lament: her nation invaded,
> enemies on the rampage, bodies in piles,
> slavery and abasement. Heaven swallowed the smoke.

In his luminous introduction, which is as much a gift to the reader as the translation itself, Heaney allows us to take a sneak view into the translator's workshop. He had taken up the work on *Beowulf* and abandoned it again because it was 'scriptorium-slow'. However he returned to it finally because, consciously or not, Anglo Saxon metrics and alliterative rhymes had been informing his own poetry: 'Part of me . . . had been writing Anglo-Saxon from the start'. Anglo-Saxon, he felt, was 'his voice-right' as much as the Irish language which, as he discovered during his studies of the history of English, sprang both from the same source. The fact that the Irish word *uisce* and the name of the river Usk in Britain for example had the same etymology delighted him: 'in my mind the stream was suddenly turned into a kind of linguistic river of rivers . . ., a riverrun of Finnegans Wakespeak pouring out of the cleft rock . . . The Irish/English duality, the Celtic/Saxon antithesis were momentarily collapsed.' Heaney found with the Old English word *tholian*, which, in the form of *thole* i.e. bear without wrath is still in use in the North of Ireland, another exemplar of a word that bridged cultural partitions. One might even go further back and, looking at Gothic *thulan*, German *dulden*, Swiss *dolen*, Danish *taale*, Latin *tolerare*, Greek *talao*, all of which have the same meaning of to bear, to tolerate, speculate on a pre-Babylonian 'Ur-river' in which all European languages were united. But as Walter Benjamin warns in his essay on the task of the translator, in spite of the apparent kinship of languages their intent is not the same. As much as I admire Heaney's translation of Beowulf, I have to confess that I feel a certain unease when confronted with the Germanic heroic past. It has been sullied by the Nazis for my generation and generations to come. The leader and his loyal warriors are disturbingly reminiscent of the Fuhrer — who incidentally loved posing as a dragon-slayer in shiny armour — and his underlings. Ties of blood, strong leadership, unquestioning obedience, a military mindset — these were essential parts of Nazi ideology as against a pluralist, multi-ethnic, modern industrial society. Most unsettling of all are the memories of racist Nazi propaganda awakened by the treatment of the descendants of Cain:

> Grendel was the name of this grim demon
> haunting the marshes, marauding around the heath
> and the desolate fens; he had dwelt for a time
> in misery among the banished monsters,
> *Cain's clan, whom the Creator had outlawed*
> *and condemned as outcasts. For the killing of Abel*
> the Eternal Lord had *exacted a price.*
> Cain got no good from committing that murder
> because the Almighty made him *anathema*
> and out of the *curse of his exile* there sprang
> ogres and elves and evil phantoms
> and the giants too who strove with God
> time and again until he gave them their reward.
>   (Italics mine)

With impure intent, the Nazis exploited the epics for their perverted purposes and, for many of us, the pseudo-mythological terminology of ardent nationalism and heroism, of tribe, nation, blood, loyalty and obedience has forever been poisoned. Of course it's not the responsibility of the ancient epic that the passage about Cain's clan uncomfortably echoes the language of racism used by the Nazis against the Jews (Christ killers, marauders, outcasts, cursed with exile etc.) to isolate them. But it does throw a light on the timelessness of the mechanism of exclusion: it is the other group's banishment from all social interaction which in turn is used as an argument to justify their destruction. Bearing the troubled relationship Germans have with things Germanic in mind it's unthinkable that poets like Grass or Enzensberger would ever turn to the sagas with anything other than an ironic or deconstructive purpose.

However, on this other bank of the linguistic river it still seems possible to translate *Beowulf* without ulterior motives or too many scruples, and that one of the greatest poets in the English language has lovingly and convincingly done so is proof of an enviable innocence and purity of intent, and we should be sincerely grateful to him.

Eva Bourke

In Duiche Iar

The fields were no larger than the green envelops
our dead-and-gone Greek teachers used
to post obloquies to our parents.

We climbed stone walls, got lost in a maze.
Round every corner we feared the minotaur
might come thrashing through brambles

but, as luck would have it, we met face to face
only the serene local bull,
a youngster with six female dependants.

In Duiche Iar light dripped, rocks and tarmac
glittered from thousands of punctures,
the mountains were studded with pinpoints of silver.

Thigh deep in marsh reeds we watched the Atlantic
turn over once once more on its back.
I don't know why the crows reminded me of seminarians,

maybe because they were huddled together,
celibate and black, in the one tree
not blown back to front by the storm

which crashed in raging against a bolted gate
somewhere beyond the hills,
bundled us through the graveyard

where the dead in their coffin ships
were slowly sinking towards bedrock.
We were amazed at an old sand stealer

who with his donkey was busy rearranging the planet,
a job more futile, we thought,
than that of King Sisyphus.

On Duiche Iar strand the sea rolled up
the scroll with its signature in fresh blue ink,
left urchin shells dotting the shore

white as fairy skulls and as bald,
we could see the stitch holes of elfin embroidery
where their needlework was unpicked.

In Duiche Iar we discovered dogs own six senses or more
and all the boreens. One appeared to us
out of thin air, tailed us wherever we went

to shield us from harm, barked at anything
that moved, our shadows, the neighbour's labrador,
a tractor rattling past. We knew well

we couldn't take a step without her
and submitted, counting our blessings,
this windfall of kindness on such rocky ground.

Let our companions on our travels always
be like her with her wind-blown coat
in true local colour, black and white,

her tilted left ear and her dissimilar eyes,
one a deep liquid brown,
the other blue and changeable as her native sea.

Her dark eye saw a future wrought with danger,
her blue eye looked into a world
where metamorphoses were commonplace as rocks,

gods walked on hindlegs, stars fell into tin pails
and the ends of the earth
rested on the shoulders of mongrels.

Eva Bourke

Travels with Gandolpho

Do you recall our trip south?
We lay on wooden benches,
ate dried squid from paper bags.
Fields of chillies carpeted the ground
flaming red all the way to the train tracks.
I was aflame, thought of nothing but you.

Time was called — or was it night?
on a dark station platform
below signal posts that someone told us
had been makeshift gallows
they'd hung partisans from during the war.
A kind soul hosed us down,

we drank topaz-coloured wine.
Music came flooding from the wireless,
cantabile, sostenuto.
Handfuls of anise from Nîmes,
light brown mouse droppings.
Can you still see the horses in the arena,

their raised eyebrows and soft eyes,
their curling nostrils?
Would the world be palatable without such airs
and graces?
The prosaic bulls clanked
and jangled inside the stables,

and we drank the bitterest coffee
our worthless money could buy.
The afternoon buzzed with prophetic gadflies.
Grandmother, in the heart of winter,
in her forget-me-not apron,
hesitated between pantry door

and tulip bed. In earthenware jugs
yellow dill feathers bloomed
She'd almost paid with her life
for the recipe on those long crooked steps
in Odessa. (Years later we tasted the same essence
in a Polish dive east of Notre Dame.)

The hot white liquor with the strange ingredient
made me throw up in the funicular.
You, Gandolpho, held my forehead.
I never loved you as much.
The children below by the river
were jumping in as if it were their future.

Deirdre Brennan

June

Here toadflax sleeps in crannies of old walls
Dandelions embed themselves in every cleft
Hedge mustard roots at a lamp-post's base;
Uncompromising weeds establish dynasties
As earth sprouts and spatters her ancient seeds.

You and I control well cultivated plots
Where roses that for more than half the year
Pruned back in beds to spiky skeletons
Just now discharge great cabbages of bloom
That snag and bleed thoughts barely fingered.

Something from every luscious June we ever knew
Absentmindedly nuzzles the senses
Until each inch of us seeps cerulean
And we tie and stake forgotten flowers
To the musk and damask of memory.

These, opiates that sustain our days
Absorb us into vortices of such sweetness
That evenings find us like fossilised bees,
The last nectar of our summer honey-sacked,
Grown quite solid in stony abdomens.

Deirdre Brennan

The Last Observance

Here where the land ends
in a scattering of islands,
small stone-walled fields
cowering away from the sea,
light trembling behind rain,
we vigil by drenched rocks,
an eye on the turning tide,
waiting for you to decide
when it is time to move
in the last observance.

Gulls spill from the sky when
like a priestess, bare-footed,
in your black waxed jacket,
you step forward to prise open
what might be a lunch-box
except it holds the ashes
of your six-foot-tall father
borne by you to the Atlantic
all the way from a cattle farm
north of Brisbane.

I, who never saw the ashes
of the dead before, avert my eyes
not to intrude on your leave-taking,
study seaweed on the rock-line,
imagine to shape the man that was,
clavicle, femur, tibia and rib,
a tumult of bones I cannot name
and when I look again you are
already casting him on the tide

and it is whipping him to cream,
a galaxy of particles eddying,
whirling away from each other,
carried off before our eyes

beyond the shallows,
tugged by undercurrents
through channels between islands
to bed down with the bones of fish
and bird, niche between the eggs
of toadfish, lodge in a dog-whelk's shell.

This, his last wish, fulfilled,
you say neither hymn nor
prayer for him but turn, face wet
with spray and tears, seeing
the long centuries of drowned stars
and moons like tabernacle lamps
hanging fathoms deep over him
and all of a sudden, you are longing
for home, the Pacific blue as a bird's egg,
the comfort of an opposite sun.

D. Nurkse

The Stray

A small white terrier,
muzzle bluish with snow,
followed me among the graves.
When I paused to read an inscription —
blessed are the dead
which die in the Lord —
it stopped to raise one leg

then gazed expectantly
as if my cloud of breath
were a balloon in a comic.
We climbed toward that hill
at whose crest my father lies

and the mutt gambolled stiffly
in and out of my boot prints,
staring up with mild eyes
glossy with cataracts.
When we came to Gabriel

I commanded: *Stay.*
It plopped on its haunches,
watching me recede
until I couldn't stand it.
I turned and shouted: *Heel*
and the echo came
from the granite mouth:
Heal.

John Knowles

The Fulcrum

Careful of arms and legs
as I lift this barely 10 pound weight,
so many bags of sugar
(it's always sugar),
what comes back to me
is not so much the sense
of this still too fragile body
that I gather so closely
to myself,
but something almost like
an altered gravity,
an unaccustomed strength.

Five years ago
in the labour ward
what I remember is the twisted fuselli
of the umbilical cord before the cut,
the afterbirth,
a midwife holding our son
upside down by the heels,
the face flying out of him,

but still
this same sense
of a sudden shift in things,
as if I'd found that fulcrum
of Archimedes
on which a world could be lifted.

Jean O'Brien

The Angels

My father took a spade and buried them
at the bottom of the garden — the woman's voice
explained. Listening with half an ear,
I paused — they were still born, came early,
not properly formed, she said.
You couldn't lay them in a cemetery back then.

I looked from the window at my own garden,
holding no more than the bones of family pets.
In Autumn dividing the border plants,
I hear my spade hit and hope it's a stone
and not the remains of the many cats interred there.

This woman talking; her voice a scalpel
of sound, has children at the bottom of her garden.
Bundles hidden under the clay,
no headstones, no coffins, just an abundance
of flowers, blue forget-me-nots and bitter rue,
for no-one could ever dig there.

I turn back to my work, in a silence of glass,
the radio quiet now, and note my young daughter
turning the stones at the bottom of our garden,
her own little cairn. I've told her that fairies live there.

Merryn Williams

Charlotte's Baby

I dreamed my sisters came back, but they looked different,
fashionably dressed, and they were poking fun at me.
It was worse than when they died, because then I could hope
for a happy reunion.   Now I have no sisters.

My window overlooks a great sea of ancient
chest-tombs, where the six of us sat in bright weather
eating our crusts.   Scarlet fever, tuberculosis
cut swathes through our parish, but I have a second chance.

I know my baby is a girl; she hasn't quickened
but I can feel her weightless skeleton, cradled in my
bloodstream.
The old women say that if you are sick repeatedly
(as I have been this week) it's a girl, and healthy.

I'll name her Emily, Anne, Marie, Elizabeth;
we'll read and sew by firelight; I'll talk French with her.
I hardly remember those years of producing books
instead of children.   This is a new chapter.

Today I walked as far as the waterfall, swollen
with melted snow, raging in winter power,
and light sprang out, though it was wild and cloudy,
in flashes, as on that day we saw three suns.

I want her to live; I know I shall be glad when the nausea
recedes.   My clothes are drenched, but the heavy rain
has cleared and left the western sky faint yellow
like a starved crocus, forcing it way through the last snow.

Mary Wickham

Foot

Le pied de ma tante it was that undid me.
Restraint and necessity had shored up grief's demands
until the sight of a bare foot,
nonchalantly hanging, crossed over its mate,
its owner reading Saturday's paper.
It had the perfection of milk skin that foot,
but betrayed its age in the joint of the big toe,
which carried the distortions of long use
and the child's memory of ill-fitting previously-used shoes.

I said, *I am going to see her.*
I want to see her once more in time,
before tomorrow's crowd.
It had been two days since she left home,
taken by the grey men.
I wanted, bizarrely, to make sure she was okay in the flesh,
   to see her safe.
Of her spirit there was no doubt.
So we all went, my father, my brothers and I.

I looked at her face;
I looked at her hand;
Touched both in the peach-light
of a music synthetic yet soothing.
She looked not so much peaceful as noble,
resolute you might say,
dressed in her favourite suit.
Drawing back the white satin lining of the box
I looked at her shoeless feet.
She would have been pleased the grey men brought us cups of
tea.

Months later it was my aunt's like foot which brought my
mother back to me
and set flowing my ample tears.

Patrick Moran

Birthplace

She is growing old:
stretchmarked from years of tillage,
seeding, reaping.

Her expanded pastures
bearing scars of surgery
on vibrant hedges.

Her summer finery,
her fragrance subdued by toxic
deodorants.

In winter, shivering
in ruts, unsheltered ditches;
passing fouled waters.

Her memory is fading:
each funeral, each shut-up house
just more dead brain cells. . .

Her past is as real now
as sepia-tinted photos
of a vanished era:

birdsongs opening
on dog-rose and whitethorn;
her pristine streams,

her unshorn tresses;
the haycocks rising,
dome-like, in her aftergrass.

Patrick Moran

Faith Healer in Age

With her high-boned, sunken cheeks
And straggly hair, she might be
Just another aging spinster,

Were it not for her nunnish eyes;
Her hands so meekly joined;
And, despite her welcoming me,

The way her chat keeps lapsing
As if she were retreating
To an inner sanctum.

No, only the scattered old
Are left to testify
To the cures she wrought.

There's no anthology
Of BEFORE and AFTER
Photos to show how skin

Was cleared of ringworm's
Hideous, spreading lesions;
Shingles, rashes, eczema.

There are not tabloid headlines
To storm indifference,
To blare our MIRACLE!

Nor am I still the boy
Who came here years ago
To be cured of tetters;

Who wondered, meeting her,
If she lived on morsels,
Sacrificed sleep for prayer;

The boy who, in the dim light,
Watched her removing relics
From their satin cases

Before applying them
To the diseased flesh
In a trance of litanies;

Who wriggled in her gaze;
Who felt like fleeing, but
Stayed rooted to the spot.

Howard Wright

Warm Milk

An incident way back cursed their reputation,
how they covered your face in childhood,
their telepathy unnerving you, seeing right
through you, reading your mind with emerald eyes.

First to go were the kittens swelling the river
in their bags of stones; and now the mother paws
the back door — edgy, pushy, over-anxious —
and you disappear under the stairs to fetch,

Something she would like. She is still whinging
for food and drink and her tumbling brood
when you open your hand with an hypocritical smile,
and something dubious warms the milk.

Pádraig Ó Snodaigh

The Handsomest Man in Ireland

James Simmons, *The Company of Sinners*, Salmon, £7.99.

Simmons can always be depended upon to annoy: from his *Honest Ulsterman* days he has been athwart (and that is descriptive only, neither derogatory nor laudatory) any given consensus. And that is a good.

Sometimes there might seem to be an excess of libidinous enthusiasm: all that prancing. . . 'on the sofa and sideboard and the woodstore' in 'Homage to Longfellow', from this present, attractively produced collection, is one possible annoyer.

All writers do, naturally, echo and use, to be part of, reflect the experiences of others: not all will defend the naming as Simmons does in his often moving 'Winter Wedding'.

> They say poetry can hurt,
> you shouldn't be probing
> your friends' lives,
> But insight isn't killing,
> imagined truth heals
> real or imaginary wounds
> with its own means
> or spills away
> in its inaccuracy.

Maybe he is best in the occasional accidental encounter, as in 'A Blessed Transaction', with a bank teller in Larne:

> He said, 'I come from near there,
> Keady.' He wasn't testing me.
> 'That's Sarah Makem country, isn't it?'
> It was nice for something genuine to stir
> over a bank counter. A great singer
> that not everyone knows, nodded towards,
> that she might bless, for once,

> a money transaction, and linger
> over lives apparently powerless
> to improve anything. I smiled
> as he then smiled and nodded, 'yes'.

or in the echo from a shared archetypic past:

> but your loud music lacks the breath
> of my three men's sweet harmonies.
>
> They sang as lovely as the sea;
> if Neisha was the wave's bass groan,
> then Anle was the tenor wind,
> Ardan the good ship's baritone.
> I loved those limbs that my limbs pressed,
> his body like a white birch tree
> at quiet daybreak as he dressed,
> his strength and grace and modesty.
>
> Come, great King Conor, foolish, greedy,
> come to my wooden arms and thrash,
> come to the garden, muddy, weedy.
> come to the burnt fire, taste the ash.
>
> — 'Deirdre's lament for Neisha'

or in the rage from particular experiences that have perennial meaning

> I am tired of old randy conmen,
> the bishops and kings and their frantic
> henchmen, and also revolutionaries —
> would-be-kings-bustling for place.
> Welcome to sound humane committee men
> making the best of our existing laws,
> wherever they may be.
>
> They were not at Coleraine,
> where the bureaucracy fought the teachers
> and won. They are not on our Arts Council,
> which used to be a safe haven for skint artists,
> like the BBC. In my time they grew proud
> and bureaucratic and corrupt.

> You had to touch your hat
> to win a share of the public money thay had to dispense...
> — 'Supporters'

but best of all, perhaps in the life and death and hope of 'The Royal Victoria Hospital, Children's Operating Theatre' where the move from the generalised statement to the real, poignant personal is powerful.

> ... Surgeons don't need to justify the work they do;
> their flesh cutting and bone-breaking
> is always the opposite of cruelty and killing.
> They can seem our only heroes, skilled and caring
> against nature's blunders. Overbearing
> and vain maybe; but I know they weep
> over their mistakes, uneasy sleepers.
> If they were cold as charity,
> who would I be to blame their manners, or query
> their taste in murals? Whatever glamour
> attaches to surgeons is earned, their failures
> and great feats are serious. One mistake
> is a family's unredeemable heartbreak.
> One victory tonight and we can keep
> our baby, and touch the surgeon's gown, and sleep.

In 'Last Things' he says:

> There's something in me, as in Frank O'Connor,
> that gets backs up. The politics of literature!
> Half Irish mafia and half tourist trade.
> Frost said, 'Take something like a star
> to stay our minds on and be staid.
>
> Take something like a bear... and be afraid.

He has never been that — in print at any rate, and if there is no great comfort for him in always being athwart, the rest of us can celebrate his independence.

Paul Perry

Sundays

First, you had to wear your Sunday best,
say a stiff navy blue shirt, ironed trousers,
slacks your father called them. Your shoes
you had to polish. You and your brothers

bent over in the kitchenette, your mother
said utility room, rubbing the old yellow rag
over the football worn leather,
the laces you tried not to pull too tight

made brittle by winter's shrug. Next you would have
to find your father's keys, lost, misplaced,
hidden. A frantic escapade under cushions
and clocks where you stood about looking

in places twice, thinking already about the end
of mass, hoping he wouldn't catch you idling
and when the keys, sacrosanct themselves, were found
and you didn't have to help pour a kettle of steaming

water onto the frost inscribed windscreen of the car
you crowded into the back-seat where the ascetic sting
of his after-shave waited with the thin lips
of his impatience. Your mother was giving it, mass,

a miss, this week. Later, when you became an altar
boy, you were seduced by the language of faith:
the sacristy, a mysterious and alluring word you
relished like tabernacle or liturgy, cold on the tongue

like iron. Chalice had the reassuring inflection
of an austere dawn and all the authority and apparent
order that incited reverence like the chilling command
of a parent, as if the words were a punishment you were
    thankful for.

Men shuffled from foot to foot
at the back of the church like cattle

trying to shake the musty dank of their breed,
restless for the other public houses to open.

The wind hustled its way
through the open doors upsetting the tranquillity
of the candle flames where old women knelt.
You shuffled your way into the heavy oak pews

and sat and stood according to the priest's directions,
all the time looking at the girl in the seat in front of you,
her bare supple neck revealed as something
blessed and while St. Paul wrote to the Corinthians

you thought about devouring the flesh before you.
And then there hung poor Jesus on the cross alone.
When it came time to take communion
you mulled over whether to take it in your hand

or directly into the mouth and once you had overcome
that one quandary you worried over how not to sink
your teeth into the body of Christ, something your brother
told you would send you straight to you know where.

It felt strange to have swallowed his body,
to have consumed the son of god,
to implicate yourself in something which sounded like a crime,
transubstantiation.

Outside the church after mass
your father gave you money, a pile of dirty coins,
to buy the newspapers and you waded home
with the headlines smearing your fingers with ink

and after dinner, maybe your grandparents were along,
before your father settled into his arm-chair,
you wondered briefly
what it was he might have prayed for,

whether he thought about Jesus alone on the cross,
whether he, too, was afraid of the dark
when the heavy oak doors of the church closed
and the candles, with a quiet gasp, were quenched.

Paul Perry

Blessed is the Fruit

Desolate apples, hold
tight in your bowl of water,
red, blushing, and blossoming light;

too big for the fruit bowl,
bitter pie stuff,
clean and eager

like some dowdy buoys
in a storm,
on say a Sunday,

and we wearing
our costumes,
not for mass,

but Halloween,
my brother remember is
something Frankensteinian

and I'm a ghost
dunking my head
into the cold

frivolous water
mouth open
like a dumb fish

in the depths —
childhood game;
apples, storm lights,

biblical beacons
of a lost faith,
first fruits, un-

forbidden, but lost
like round unanchored
islands where we

returned after walking
from house to house
and trundling to and from the bonfire

to where the bowl,
like two clapsed
plastic pale green hands,

a memory turned over,
lay with its bitten and chewed,
that is the yellowing skin of apple flesh

swelling sadly into the soft
unforgiven pulp
of all consumed

and discarded
temptations, though this
was the first, the first I remember.

Greg Delanty

The Scalding

'A'ole kanawai ma keia wahi!'

I'd stay after Lenten mass till time to trudge up Turner's
Cross,
    a pizawn, lugging my mála of bricks to school's purgatory.
I prayed to be a saint, committing miracles as often
    as impure thoughts. I sought to comfort the poor
and infirm, offering my lunch to the bully Alex Casey,
    eagerly assisting broken-armed Lily Walsh.
Long past lights out I pored over *Lives of the Saints*
    with my Woolworth's torch as others read the *Rover*,
Wizard or *Wonder Woman*, unafraid of sacrificing my sight,
    albeit I feared blindness zealously performing Onan.
I preached to seagulls in from the Blackash, lip read goldfish,
    yapped with stray cats and dogs. After my nature project
collaged the minute-by-minute extinction of plants,
    animals and birds, I switched to the other Francis
like a football fan who divines his star is over the hill.
    As Francis Xavier, my uncorrupted body returned to
the Goa of Cork and the city flocked round my glass coffin.
    After losing my weekly shilling and Anthony left me
broke,
in a huff, I signed up on Saint Brendan's curragh.
    But my real idol, even if he was merely in the halfpenny
venerable league, was the leper lover, Damien of Molokai.

Never one for half measures, I prayed to be another Damien,
    exile
    among exiles, giving succour and mending the wanton
ways
of the living dead, men and women dulling their plight,
losing
    themselves in what was glossed as bodily whims
(which secretly had us all curiously, if only dimly, envious).
    In preparation for my island I trained myself to bear
the walking dead's putrefying stench by taking deep breaths

    every time Jim Slattery slipped off his shoes under the desk,
and held tough as the whole Palace shrank from the lepers in
Ben   H*ur.*
   The terror thrilled as we gasped at those sackcloth creatures
with noseless faces, suppurating eyes, and stumps for hands.
   They grovelled out of caves darker than the confessional,
their bell-ringing scarier than the Monday morning school bell.
   I pestered my mother for sewing tips, intent as Damien
to dignify lepers and outfit a band to accompany funerals,
   fashioning drums, pipes and fifes from rusty kerosene cans.
Musicians, often missing three or four fingers, miraculously
   turned into maestros, backed by the harmony of sea and surf.

A school missionary told us the story, how the leper priest
   mistakenly poured boiling water on his flesh and feeling no
pain, smiled and nodded to himself. The carried-away visitor
   addressed the class congregation, as Damien addressed
his flock next morning, almost joyously, with "We lepers".
   He spoke of another strain— name it *macrobacterium leprae*—
the bacilli of complicity carried in our food and clothes,
   in hidden seams of our varied regular lives, sewn by
the world's less fortunate hands, unseen as Molokai's lepers;
   how really we're all lepers, even if we are dismissive
like that woman who, as Damien stepped onto the island, cut off
her finger, turned her back and derisively flung it over
her shoulder. The missionary surveyed us querying: "Do we nod
   and smile to ourselves? Had we spilled the scalding water?"
He exhorted us all to go out, hereafter, into the world as Damiens.

Balmy as it sounds, I never quite shook off that sermon, but feel,
    at best, like Damien's crotchety attendant
watching the pot bubble on the stove, tired of being kept late,
    setting the steaming kettle down before I sign off.

Louis de Paor

Focaldeoch
i gcuimhne Iain Mhic an Ghobhainn

Bhíos ag cur síos dó ar fhear Inis Cara
a chuir saothar seanBhíobla ar fhocail,
a chuir turraing aibhléise
le huisinn na teanga
nó gur labhair an eitinn
is an Uimhir Dhé
ar leathscamhóg as béal a chéile.

Bhí babhlaí briste is conamar cainte
scaipthe romhainn sa tslí
o Mhaigh Cuilinn go Ros Cathail,
gléas on ngrian ar chlogad a chinn
is a bhlaosc chomh maol le muga cré
i suíochán an bháis lem ais.

Bhí an t-am ag scinneadh tharainn
ar luas gluaisteáin ón tSeapáin,
fallaí fuara scoite aige cheana ina cheann
dom thabhairt leis siar
leathchéad bliain go dtí Oileán Leodhais
mar ar bhrúigh béal na baintrí
lus mínáireach an chromchinn faoi chois
chomh diongbháilte le téacs seanTiomna.

Chuir sí de gheasa air, dá mhéid a íota,
gan deoir a bhlaiseadh i gcroit ná i mbothán
mar a raibh fríd an ghalair á cuisniú
ag miasa is mugaí scoilte,
tinneas ina ráfla mailíseach á scaipeadh
chomh huilechumhachtach dofheicthe
le trócaire Dé ar thairseach an tsaoil.

Ag teacht thar reilig Uachtair Aird
bhí a chuimhne chosnocht á réabadh
ag clocha a sciobadh ó Theach na mBocht,

bhí sruthán buí an phailin
ag déanamh meala ar uaigh de Bhailís,
eascoin aibhléise ag glinniúint ar a bhais
is a chroí is a chraiceann breicneach
á scoilteadh mar mhias athláimhe

Lá brothaill, adúirt sé, i dtigh comharsan,
dhein cnaipe domlais dá chroí ina bhéal
nuair a chonaic frithchaitheamh a amhrais féin
chomh soiléir le teastas báis
ar aghaidh na mná cneasta
ar eitigh sé muga leamhnachta as a láimh

Tá mo scornach ata le tart
ag triall arís ar bhothán tite a dháin
go bhfaighead i measc na ngréithre briste
blas éigin den uaisleacht chráite
ná maireann sa tsaol níos mó,
an soiscéal de réir Iain
a leigheasfadh íota mo chroí.

Gospel
i.m. Iain Crichton Smith

I was telling him about the man in Inis Cara/ who made words
work hard as an old Bible,/ who sent electric shocks/ through the
temples of language/ until tuberculosis and the binary number/
spoke as one voice with damaged breath.// Broken bowls and shards
of talk/ were scattered before us on the road/ from Moycullen to
Roscahill,/ the sun glinting on the helmet of his head/ bare as a cup/
in the death-seat beside me.// Time skidded past us/ like a Japanese
car and already/ he was clearing stone walls in his head/ taking me
with him/ fifty years back to the Isle of Lewis/ where the widow's
words/ trampled the shameless daffodil/ with the certainty of a
lesson from the Old Testament.//She made him promise,/ whatever
his thirst not to touch/ a drop in any croft or cottage/ where a hint
of disease might have lodged/ in cracked mugs or dishes,/as sickness
spread like a vicious rumour/ all-powerful and invisible/ as God's
mercy on the threshold of the world.// As we passed the cemetery at

Oughterard/ a yellow stream of pollen/ honeyed the headstone of Colm Wallace,/ his barefoot memories were gashed/ by stones stolen from the ruins of the Poorhouse,/ electric eels glittered in his hands/ heart and freckled skin/ cracking like second-hand crockery.// On a sweltering day in a neighbour's house,/ he said, his heart turned to gall in his mouth/ when he saw his own uncertainty reflected/ clear as death-certificate on the woman's face/ when he refused kindness from her hands.// My throat is swollen with thirst/ as I make my way again/ to the tumbled down cottage of his poem/ hoping to find there among the broken crockery/ a taste of the hurt and gentleness/ that is no longer in the world,/ the gospel according to Iain/ that might assuage my raging heart.

Harry Clifton

Red Fox Country

I watched myself disappear
Off the bookshelves, and went away
To live them through, the invisible years.
And that is where I am today,

In red fox country, forking left
Beyond Armagh, around Lough Neagh
And through to Toome, the back way.
Spirit, intellect or gift —

For now, they have had their day,
And it calms me, this limbo
Where all, like myself, devoid of Grace
In a wilderness of symbols,

Must wait for the lights to change.
Salvation, say the walls.
And I, whose numberplates are strange,
Whose accent anyone can tell

For a lost soul, a broken heart
From the Free and Fallen State,
Must colonise my own backyard
With the hour latening,

And the fox, the interloper,
A redgold streak, running deeper
In his own country. Sam Brown belts,
A word at the window. Pelts

Of hedgehog, badger, stoat,
The terrible rictus of the slain
On the straight and narrow. Wave me on
To a life beyond Dungannon,

A life beyond Cookstown, Moneymore,
Where true redemption starts.
A human house. A wind off the Shore.
And a woman from these parts

— *Deirdre, Deirdre, sandman's daughter,
Tonight let us lie, like oil on water* —
Sheltering me, with a broken gamp
And the yolk of a hurricane-lamp

As I fall asleep at the wheel
With red fox country all around,
Ever less visible, ever more real,
Running myself to ground.

Peter Sirr

The Hunt

Where were we? As if we had dived
into the city's dreaming, tumbled
from strange nook to stranger cranny
as the year darkened

Mountbrown   Old Kilmainham
adrift in a hollow, gaunt stone
above the Camac   Lady's lane
a murky glamour, cottages out of nowhere

We crossed a threshold
Rivals in the bedroom sniffed the air
investors in the kitchen
calculated rental income

We stayed a little, out of sight
melting into the furniture
we were pioneers in a deep interior
hungry ghosts among the Horlicks jars

We drifted through the intimate city
like dust, like light
settling briefly, silent but alert
looking for an opening

What relief to be out
in sun and early dark
greeting the brickwork
of Sitric street and Ivar street

or plunging eastward
canal water and stadium dusk
a shine of swans on the bank
the grey gash of a railway bridge

At 4.30 pm, the light withdrawn
the whole place pulled its chair
closer to the table
muttering secrets of itself

Skaldbrother
loped home with the booty
a crowd shifted outside the jail
old bones stirred

The poor   the triumphant
the pigkiller   the hanged
came out   We returned late
dust of centuries in our hair

old coins in our pockets
Tomorrow we'll spend them
A light long handled
will warm the brick again

Peter Sirr

China

There's a moment the air will thicken and the light shift, as if
another country has poured itself in, another life
lent its corona   and suddenly the stars are here, milk spills
across the heavens; whoever you are ripples, splits, multiplies,
whatever there is flickers before your eyes
and if slowly the planet diminishes, if finally the ground
steadies under your feet and the spinning tongues resolve
into the one sentence in the one place, you'll still walk
with giant feet, still fall through the air, still speak
as if a shadow lengthened across the language

or it will happen like this:
a sudden, butchery odour on the street
and the pavement opens, the sky parts, something
floating back with such clarity it pulls you short
an old early morning, your hands slipped back and falling
into your mother's, a few yards of strange brightness,
first a green shop then a blue, a clock striking overhead
and then it's gone, then a blur, the rest of the journey
irrecoverable. What did it want? Nothing more than to say
this particular moment is on its own track, in its own time,
and if you should fall sideways into it, fall gladly

or you are staring out the window, going nowhere,
you are patrolling the gardens of China
and a shrub will open its bright door, a certain
aspect of gravel, a tender tilt of the planet
                                             yet
how foolish to have imagined otherwise, to have thought
our abandoned selves would not go on without us, quite
  unconcerned,
not to have noticed the small army marching beside us, on its
  way
to China, to Lipton's for groceries, to portal after portal.
We could be there now, loafing on stars, on a hammock
hung from days, watching the light

that lends us to the future and sometimes calls us back
and sometimes washes through us whatever it has touched, a
    drift
that settles in our bones, that tells us
we can no more live singly than light can fall on one place
only.

Colette Connor

Redemption

Time is torture to those who dwell on time,
forever replaying the last scene,
the last shot in focus,
unblurred by memory.

So we manage our pain,
Dressing it up in garish garb,
seeking for some contrivance
to save us pondering the past.

The old remedies are gone,
no use calling on chalk idols,
they are mute and cannot return
our protestations of love.

Nothing but silence
to turn up the volume on trooping thoughts,
the march of guilt on gravel
playing havoc with the brain.

All memory is pain,
even the gladness,
only the desire for redemption still burns,
the hope that our ghosts grow familiar in time.

Denise Blake

Rathlin Island

Five hundred left in one day,
stepped from this small island
onto a waiting coffin ship;
when the fungus seeped
through potato starch,
spreading the stench of death.

Wind over the waves raises steam
like breath on a cold window pane.
The cliffs are ridged from fingernails
clawed down the black earth
as their thoughts tried to climb home.
White dust on the shore is their ashes.

Out in the water a rock
has worn down into a giant foot
taking its first step away;
in its centre is a stake,
as in a crucifixion,
holding it to the Rathlin.

Ronald Tamplin

To Drive a Wise Man Mad

*Surtout, rime une version
Sur le mal des pommes de terres!* - Rimbaud

I was to do a review of Irish Guide Books,
June 1847. Do you remember?
It was a Vision of Connaught in the Nineteenth
Century. *Sow diligently, for there will be
Men to reap, whether with sword or sickle. The sun
Is not yet so dark, nor is the moon only blood,
Though the madness knocks at the skull.* Lie down beside
The pool, watch the cascading stream, and separate
The sounds you hear; water, insects and the mountain
Birds. And the silence there. In which you hear your pulse.

The evening grass is damp. The flowers of the thorn
Are heavy on the air this year. The sun sets red
Above the sleeping sea. Over there, the cluster
Of cabins where two years ago I ate well, salt
And potatoes, with the man, his wife and children.
They spoke in Irish, nothing of 'enlightenment,'
'The modern,' 'progress' and 'the masses.' The Nineteenth
Century would not know itself and could not speak.

There is no light, no smoke from the chimneys, nor smell
Of turf. There is a smell. Like Golgotha, it lies
Upon the air. Grass grows before the doors. They hang
Open or unhinged. Two gaunt dogs cringe from me. They
Howl. These are the cabins of the dead. How have they
Lived since their master died? I stop on the threshold.
'God save all here,' I say. No voice. Was the man on
'Public work,' designed to do nothing, digging holes,
Breaking roads, leaving things worse than they were before?
And the pay would not keep them. Instead of dying
In December, was it to make them wait till March?
Their bodies shrinking as their minds thickened, voices
Cracking in their throats, brought to beg and steal, their
blood

A thin, chill serum. If you prick them, they will not
Bleed. At last they stay home to die, malice between
Them. The children dead weeks before, in scrabbled graves
Too shallow for a box. Were there scraps, they would tear
Each other for them, until in the misted dream
Of the driven mad, they die, strangers.
                                                                My throat clogs.
Hysterica passio. I stumble out. The moon
Is blood. Who I am I forget. And the way back.

This poem is one of a sequence of poems 'Fourteen Notes for John Mitchel'. The poems derive from passages in Mitchel's *Jail Journal*, and in the case of the poem 'To Drive a Wise Man Mad', from an 1847 article by him in *The Nation*.

Chris Agee

Requiem

'Hitler, c'est moi.'
       — Glucksmann

Something had turned me back. Broken stone. Ochre and lime
Leaves in the pockmark of a mortarsplash. I paused

To marvel at the chaos that composed them
Impasted in hoarfrost like sperms or dead souls frozen

In the liquid oxygen of time. Then back again
To the smoothness on a mosque's threshold, a revenant

Drifting on in the first flurries of Friday afternoon,
Windless and lightweight, sifting down in grey silence,

I walk on past shawled faces in an old Yugoslav café,
Bread smells and a glimpse of loaves, jars stacked pyramidal

As in Russia, crossing Habsburg tramlines to the market stalls
Where legs and shoe leather move round the small splash

That, invisible, unsought, I wince at. Walnuts, cabbages, tangerines:
Onions, apples, peppers, honeycomb: bowls of cheese,
   sunflower seeds:

Beautiful, spartan Arcimboldo, where Sarajevo snow is falling, falling. . .
Is ash falling into the next century.

Patricia Burke Brogan

The Painting

Velasquez de Silva
prepares ochres, burnt umbers, siennas.

He half-closes his eyes.

Brush on canvas,
he places the woman in the foreground
stooped over platters of unleavened bread
and flagons of wine
on her kitchen table.

He curves her shoulders,
slants her body.

She turns her head,
begins to breathe.

Velasquez de Silva's heart races.

The woman moves again,
watches through the serving-hatch,
as the stranger breaks bread
with men he met on the road.

She murmurs, 'He is risen.'

Velasquez de Silva
opens his eyes,
says, 'Deo Gratias'.

Bernard O'Donoghue

Two Fiddlers at Scully's

For the higher notes, the fiddle lifts Tim Browne
By the chin clean off his seat, like a child
Hoisted by the jowls to see France or China.
But not painfully: you can tell that
By the small smile that never leaves his mouth
And the readiness to laugh behind his glasses.
Raymond hardly stirs: his eyes never shift
From his fiddle which he scrutinizes
In solemn puzzlement, nudging the music out
While Browne pulls it gallantly across himself.

Maurice Harmon

Frozen Phoenix

There are moments like that
when the tongue sticks in the throat's bell
never to fall free again.

Never to sound the arlarm or the all clear.
The blocking source the frail rigging
of the mosquito net in the merciless spasm.

The lift and suck at the mothering core.
Never to be meshed in words,
stopped in mid-gulp.

When the father's dark hands
clapped the eyes across,
his breath hot on his son's neck.

Moments like that warp speech
and words that ought to clear
and cleanse knot in the throat.

From an incident in *The Temple of the Golden Pavilion* by Yukio Mishimo

Maurice Harmon

Shunkan

There was no thought of fighting the waves.
They pulled the ground from under him
and pushed the sea around him, true blue
and streaked with white caps, pushed it
firmly, then sent the entire rock about
until he was fixed in that hard blue,
that desolate cold blue and white.

There was no mention of Troy, he stood
watching the ship's decline.
No sounds now, no stretched cries,
no bird song, no jungle howl, no bent notes.
All the attention in eyes that strained,
scanned, imagining hands,
contracting absence in sunken depths.

There was no question of being tied to the stone.
He clambered there, holding on to a single vine,
desperate, clawed, fought through the one tree,
held down a branch, leaned out, far out,
fell when the branch broke, but groped again upright,
all yearning, sight fading, light going, ship
receding, far off, dimming, away, away.

This part of *Shunkan* was performed by the Kabuki actor, Kichiemon, at Kyoto's Minamiza Theatre in December 1997. The second stanza refers to sounds made by musicians and singers as part of the performance.

Derry O'Sullivan

Cogito Ergo Sum

Infans, mirabar:
Quis lunam inflatam
Deflavisset,
Quis solis sanguinem suxisset,
Quis nivis magis quam frumenti,
Squamas dilexisset?
Hodie autem miror:
Quis mirateur?

As a child I wondered/ Who inflated, deflated the moon,/ Who bled the sun./ Who preferred snowflakes to corncrakes —/ Now I wonder/ who wondered.

Pádraig Mac Fhearghusa

Allagar

'Scaoiltear an saighead!' a d'fhóghair an toil,
'Cá treo?' — an breithiúnas a d'fhiarthaigh.
'Fóill, fóill,' a d'éiligh an intleacht,
'Ní féidir go ngluaisfeadh?'
'Éalóm ar a mhuin,' a d'impigh an croí.

Súil agus gualainn a dhein an beart,
Cá luíonn an dairt tar éis an allagair?

'Loose the arrow,' proclaimed the will/ 'In what direction?' — judgement enquired./ 'Easy, easy,' demanded the intellect,/ 'Surely it won't fly?'/ 'Let's away upon it,' the heart implored.// Eye and shoulder have done the deed;/ Disputation over, where lies the dart?

Bríd Ní Mhóráin

I bhFothair na Manach

Phasálamar na pósaes i dTóin na Fothrach
samhaircíní is púir faille bhí ar tinneall le dúil,
má thug taibhsí na manach fé ndeara sinn
níor ligeadar faic orthu, chaochadar súil.
Ní raibh gíocs as na clocháin;
bhí an dónall dubh ina thost;
dúirís gur mé do leanbh gréine;
nóinín, osclaíonn fén solas buí.
Dá mbagródh an sliabh go dtitfeadh orainn
nó an mhuir go gclúdódh sinn
chuirfimis cluain orthu chun go bhfanfaidís socair,
— níl ionainn ach leá chúr na habhann,
atáidsean i searc a chéile
ó tháinig ann don domhan.

In the Monk's Ravine

We crushed the floor of Tóin na Fothrach/ horny primrose and sea camion./ There wasn't a stir from the beehive cells:/ if the anchorite spirits noticed us/ they played dumb, they never let on.// You said I was your child of the sun,/ a daisy opening yellow to the light./ If the mountain was to collapse upon us/ or the ocean to become our coverlet/ we'd calm them with a charm to be tranquil —// For there's naught to us but froth/ of the river, while they lust for one another/ since a beginning came into the earth.

Trans. Thomas McCarthy

Una O'Higgins O'Malley

Just God

Details have always been a pain for me,
the names and years of wines, or species of plants
or birds, or opus numbers of the music;
or recipes, or sporting teams
seldom remain —
only the fragrance, the taste, the flavour,
the marvellous 'birdness' of the creature,
the grace and courage of the players,
the sudden anguish of a cadence
or its mysterious assurance.

>   When someone speaks of God I like to hear,
>   Gods in the spare no-thingness of the deity, I mean,
>   not efforts to define, control, explain,
>   and not the endless news of the footsoldiers,
>   their holy networkings and tireless undertakings,
>   just God around, within, both them and me,
>   God in the quiet of a smile, a tear,
>   God in the freedom of abstractions,
>   in the silent grief of elephants over a dead companion
>   and in the buzzing of a sultry bee.

Art Murphy

Here and Now

You've seen them in unlikely places —
in crannies, waste land, on wall-ledges,
what you and I would call a hair's breadth,
finger-nail stuff — where they are an art form
of audacity. Colonisers of the impossible.
At ease with what is hard.

And there they make their little veins of life
by sensing moisture in air, water in rock.
They've made that their stock-in-trade
and live each wind-found location now
as second nature: ours, that is,
the rosebay and selfheal on embankments,
stonecrop and hart's-tongue on loosening walls.

Fiona Brennan

Feeding the Muse

And still
the ordinary things must be done.

I prune the small thyme bush
trying to save its younger shoots

plan how to stop the dog from walking
on the lemon-scented floor

watch the week old washing
drag along the muddy path

switch off Gaybo's radio wisdom
to sit down with pen and paper.

The young cairn trots in
from the garden,

falls into a hero's sleep
at my feet, beneath the table.

He ignores my futile efforts
at recording mundane moments.

I bend down and leave him
a tasty first draft to eat.

Manny Blacksher

The Guillotine

In school we feared the office guillotine
and grudged its dull machine-lathed length of edge
all eighteen inches of dour leverage.
More we loathed its surreptitious keen,
a pious moan to usage. We all knew
the blade, which grieved when nothing stalled its scrape
against the rule, would croon through measured rapes
of sweating mimeographs, which bled blue
and stained our fingers with suggestions cruel
and deft as wind in leaves: each digit cleft
might sing appalling lays until it taught
us all the treacherous loyalty of tools
that only work one way — that cut bereft
of care for what is right and what is not.

Cecilia McGovern

The "Coothrements"*

My childish hand
dared to risk nettles sting
and crawling slime,

searched the jagged shards
to find the pattern
in china or fair day ornaments.

Echoes of breakage,
the heart-stopping silence
until

"*marbh fhaisc ort*",*
a forgotten language
hurled its reproach

for a precious thing
awkwardly lost.

---

* Usual meaning is " bits and pieces". In Mayo, means household dump for broken objects.
*Bad cess to you!

Máire de Búrca

Om Namaha Shivaya — Honour the Divine Within You: The Gift of the Muses

> So spoke the ready-voiced daughters of great Zeus, and they cut a staff and gave it to me, a branch of blooming laurel, a thing to marvel at. And they breathed into me a godly voice that I should celebrate the things to come and the things of the past, and ordered me to sing of the race of the blessed gods that live for ever, always to celebrate them at the beginning and at the end.
>
> —*Theogony*, Hesiod

The Muse as inviolable agent of poetry, aligns the poetic with the divine. In this piece, I intend to focus on two interdependent, yet distinct forces that of Inspiration and Tradition. These two forces culminate in the sacred figure of the Muse.

In the Muse stands a teacher who licenses the poet to espouse the sacred and the spiritual, whilst all the while incorporating the material. In his essay, 'Religio Poetae', Eoghan Ó Tuairisc examines the relationship between the spiritual and the material as regards poetry. He describes the desire of the poet to make a connection, a *religio*, with that invisible reality beyond us: 'Tá an téarma seo bunaithe sa Laidin, *religare*, is é sin, nasc nó ceangal a dhéanamh idir dhá rud. . . Cad iad an dá rud a cheanglaítear ina chéile leis an *religio* seo? An dá shaol. An saol thall agus an saol abhus.'

The Muse that I envisage, compels the poet to fuse that link, Ó Tuairisc's *religio* between two worlds.

She is a chimera, an ethereal shadow. The personage the name denotes has become obscured in modern usage, but the word 'Muse' conjures up that indefinable source from which inspiration springs. Werner Jaeger tells us: 'In the older epic there was no thought of calling the poet by his name; he was simply an anonymous vehicle *for inspiration from the Muses*, carrying far and wide *the legends of ancient times*'[1]. In Jaeger's words the intersection of Inspiration and Tradition is pinpointed in the embodiment of the Muse. The Muse is the fount of Inspiration and is perceived as the chief orchestrator of the poetic act. The poet, in this instance, is open to total acceptance of her divine power. On revealing herself as supernatural interlocutor, the Muse imbues the poet with the grace of openness to poetic revelation, a faith in the creative process. The call to poetic revelation mirrors the call of the Creator God: 'for man to be able to enter into real intimacy with him, God willed both to reveal himself to man, and to give him the grace of being able to welcome this revelation of faith'[2]. Here, Poetic Revelation and Inspiration are synonymous and stir the poet to creativity. Creativity exists in the quietening of volition, a supreme detachment, not cold or colourless, which allows the fusion of a force, akin to grace, and the higher unconscious awareness of the poet to take place. It is the withdrawal of all that comprises personality — the ego, the will and the conscious self — that gives full sway to the exposition of the unconscious. In *Gravity and Grace*, Simon Weil tells us that: 'We participate in the creation of the world by decreating ourselves.' Similar principles are found in T.S. Eliot's discussion of 'Tradition and the Individual Talent': 'What happens is a continual surrender of himself as he is at the moment, to something which is more valuable. The progress of an artist is a continual self-sacrifice, a continual extinction of personality.'

Tradition is vital to Inspiration. Jaeger's statement on the '*Legends of Ancient Times*' refers, essentially, to the creative myths of the poet's native place. The Muse is keeper of what Paul Ricoeur terms the 'mythological nucleus' where 'Beyond the self-understanding of a society there is an opaque kernel which cannot be reduced to empirical norms or laws.'[3] The Muse, as guardian of Tradition, is that entity, divine in nature, which exists beyond the self-understanding of society and instructs the poet in the lessons of the 'opaque kernel'.

The poet holds these lessons of tradition, this immaterial and silent knowledge within, and he/she materialises them in expression. Ralph Waldo Emerson supports this when he says that the poet's experience 'inclines him to behold. . . facts flowing perpetually outward from an invisible, unsounded centre in himself.'[4] The Muse wills in the poet the articulation of a voice from which emanates the resonances of his/her tradition, a sonar quality, quite untranslatable, instructing the poet to sound the once 'unsounded' immateriality of his inner life wherein the divine dwells — Om Namaha Shivaya. In a 'Farewell to English', Michael Hartnett was impelled to answer centuries of tradition calling to him from an earthy manuscript;

> I sunk my hands into tradition
> sifting the centuries for words. This quiet
> excitement was not new: emotion challenged me
> to make it sayable. The clichés came
> at first, like matchsticks snapping from the world
> of work: mánla, séimh, dubhfholtach, álainn, caoin:
> they came like grey slabs of slate breaking from
> an ancient quarry, mánla, séimh, dubhfholtach,
> álainn, caoin, slowly vaulting down the dark
> unused escarpments, mánla, séimh, dubhfholtach,
> álainn, caoin, crashing on the cogs, splinters
> like axeheads damaging the wheels, clogging
> the intricate machine, mánla, séimh,
> dubhfholtach, álainn, caoin.

The Russian writer, Marina Tsvetaeva, acknowledges this compulsion to answer an inner call to expression, yet contrary to Hartnett, she gives testimony to the struggle of her will.

> Something, someone lodges in you; your hand is the fulfiller not of you but of it. Who is it? That which through you wants to be?. . . Things always chose me by the mark of my power, and often I wrote them almost against my will. Certain things of Russia wanted to be expressed and they chose me. And having given in — sometimes seeingly, sometimes blindly — I would obey, seek out of my ear some assigned aural lesson.[5]

The tell-tale sonar dimension sings of her Tradition and Russia, her land of origin. Tsvetaeva, as poet is susceptible to this arresting of a higher power, 'That which through you wants to be'. Although her will struggles initially, it relents, or in Weil's words *decreates itself,* and articulates the message divined from somewhere beyond her.

Tradition, Inspiration and the Word stand as a triadic source to the poetic act. Words resonate. The first requirement is an absolute belief in the power of the Word as the primary element. 'In the beginning was the Word:/ the Word was with God/ and the word was God.' (John 1:1) Inspiration has its etymological basis in the breath, wind, spirit — *Inspiratio.* Through the notion of the divinity of the breath combined with the divinity of the word, the process of revelation and creation makes itself known, '*and they breathed into me a godly voice*'. Ó Tuairisc describes the Word as the fundamental force, sacred in essence, which connects the *religio* between the two worlds. For him the Poet is guardian of that Word, and identifies the locus of inspiration from the other world as the time and place where the poet practises his craft with passion and intellect:

> Deirim go bhfuil an Focal bunúsach. . . gurb é an focal amháin a cheanglaíonn nasc an *religio* idir an dá shaol, go bhfuil an Focal sacrálta — gurb é an *Poeta* is cosantóir agus is aingeal coimhdeachta don Fhocal; agus am ar bith, áit ar bith, a dtéann an *Poeta* i mbun chéardaíocht an Fhocail a chleachtadh. . . le paisean a chroí is le cumas a aigne, is san áit sin agus ar an uair sin a shéideann an t-inanalú faoi ón saol eile.

The word sends from it radiations of a singular consciousness imbued with all the colours, shapes and connotations of possible meanings that selfsame word may have had before.

Words echoing the meanings and significances of a time past, emanate from the work of many contemporary Irish writers writing in both English and Irish. Although, as chronicled by many commentators, the Gaelic order suffered a terrible collapse, writers feel the cycles, resonances and 'macalla' of that order unbroken within them. The poet is a mnemonist. Mnemosyne, mother of the Muse, empowers the poet to remember an aesthetic order, its meanings, significances, its consciousness within them, demanding articulation, mánla, séimh, dubhfholtach, álainn, caoin. Forgetfulness leads to exile, remembrance to redemption. The flux of words coursing through the poetry is as a nepenthe for a past grief. This linguistic anxiety is depicted by Medbh McGuckian in her poem, 'Elegy for an Irish Speaker' when she longs for the 'deep roots' of the past, and curiously, as with Hartnett, she too has recourse to the earth as repository of tradition;

> I cannot live without
> your trans-sense language,
> the living furrow of your spoken words
> that plough up time
> Instead of the real past

> with its deep roots,
> I have yesterday

Words come, bringing with them tones of those that have gone before. Eliot, in 'Little Gidding, Part 1', speaks of this: 'And what the dead had no speech for, when living,/ They can tell you, being dead: the communication/ Of the dead is tongued with fire beyond the language of the living.' The Pentecostal force of the words of the dead fills the poet with meanings which fuse a link with the past and make a tradition which was seemingly broken take the form of a continuous whole.

As the Muse dwells in the sphere of the Divine, language, therefore, is constantly challenged to purify itself of everything in it that is limited, image-bound and imperfect if we are not to confuse our images of the Muse with our own human representations. The tendency to anthropomorphise is prevalent in the depiction of the Divine, an attempt to make what is insubstantial somewhat accessible to human conceptualisation. The figure of the Muse is based not only on the image but on the icon. Richard Kearney demonstrates that the premodern imagination censored the portrayal of human characteristics in the representation of the divine. The desire of the artist was to fix the attention of the congregation on the divine essence *beyond* the image by deflecting attention from the image itself. Kearney states that

> the common practise of portraying the eyes of Christ as expressionless was an apt symbol of the icon's primary function: to invite the onlooker to travel through the vacant regard of the image towards the suprasensible transcendence of God rather than linger at the surface level of purely human expressions and sensations (e.g. the beguiling, luminous eyes of a mortal face). In other words, the *theocentric* quality of the icon was evident in the fact that every effort was made to eschew worshipping the image itself so as to worship God *through* the image.[6]

Many feminist commentators have found the image of the female figure in the Muse highly restrictive due to the foregrounding of the female as purely emblematic or symbolic, allowing no realistic or human portrayal of women. In 'Tirade for the Mimic Muse', Eavan Boland unleashes an invective against a female figure who has not, in her mind, represented real female experience: 'I've caught you out. You slut. You fat trout. . .'

What is striking about this poem is that Boland directs her contempt at the Muse figure itself, using terms that could be considered as traditionally misogynistic. The notion of an author, the fashioner of representation, is not present in the text. She holds the Muse as wholly culpable for a female objectification and the distorted representation of women eclipsing female experience.

Depiction of the divine is exceptionally challenging, even problematic, if the potential strictures of images are to be avoided. There is an implicit acknowledgement that the Muse, as semblance of the divine, stands over and above all that is human. I maintain, therefore, that humanity, and by abstraction gender, is not the focus of representation. Hence, attention to binary oppositions, such as male/female and the socialisation encroaching on both of these biological constructs is not required.

In short, I bear witness to the Muse. On a parting note, I wish to quote from 'On Angels' by Czeslaw Milosz who affirms with conviction the existence of divine and celestial presences amongst us.

> All was taken away from you: white dresses,
> wings, even existence.
> Yet I believe you,
> messengers.

1 Werner, Jaeger, *The Theology of the Greek Philosophers*, trans. Edward S. Robinson, (London/New York: Oxford University Press, 1967) p.11.
2 New Catholic Catechism, (Dublin:Veritas, 1994) p.16.
3 Paul Ricoeur, 'Myth as bearer of Possible Worlds.' *The Crane Bag Journal, Volume 12*, (Dublin, Folens Ltd.) p.31.
4 Ralph Waldo Emerson, 'The Transcendentalist', *Essays and Lectures*, (New York: The Library of America, 1983) p.195.
5 Marina Tsvetaeva, *Art in the Light of Conscience: Eight Essays on Poetry*, trans Angela Livingstone, (London: Bristol Classical Press, 1992) p.173.
6 Richard Kearney, *The Wake of Imagination*, (London:Hutchinson, 1988) p.9.

Fred Johnston

What Heroes Are For
for Brian Wynne, Kinvara, Co. Clare

Under black weather we drive
Keeping the mountains in their blackness
To the South.

A roadsign comes up, white
And uncertain, fluttering like a weak
Heart in the wind.

Remote in a wrap of radio music,
We smoke and someone mentions
Him, off cycling to a dance.

He's gone out where wind and mind
Have agreement. He'll be at home
With his head butting the storm.

He'll push one leg down after the other,
The wheels will rotate, a turning
Mirrored in the stars.

He will get there, wherever it is,
Skipping into the yellow doorlight and
Its gift of letting go.

He'll unparcel himself in the dance,
Wheeling round on the end of a girl's
Hand to the limits of the world.

We were never like him. Our envy
Rises and filters out like smoke. Later
We learn he never left, and feel let down.

Tom French

Night Drive

I don't remember my brother having owned
a red Toyota or a rust-coloured Ford,
but in last night's dream we arranged to meet
in the cathederal carpark so he could drive me home
and, although I arrived with time to spare,

I was only in time to glimpse him driving away,
his long knees cramped up and around the wheel,
the cheerful little plumes of blue exhaust.
Later, when he passed me on the sea road,
it was dark and I was in that rage that drives you

every stop of the road home, but by the ghost-
light of the dash I could just make out his face.
He was smiling and facing me and waving as if
he knew the road so well he didn't even need
to keep his eyes on it. Then he was sitting

in our kitchen when I got back, glancing
through that day's *Independent* and chatting
with our mother who had put the frying pan
on the gas stove ring to cook his tea. She was
so delighted to be feeding him again he'd gone

so long without eating underground she wasn't
listening to me ranting and raging — '*I don't care
how long he's been gone. You don't drive off
and leave someone. It's just not fair!*'
They killed themselves laughing at that.

And when I buried the bones of my fist
in the bones of his face, and he fended off
the blows as easily as if I was a child, suddenly
I understood they understood something
that they were teaching me — that this is what

the dead do and it is just. They arrange to give
us lifts. They pass us smiling when they see us
on the road, driving cars they never owned.
They force us to make our own way home
on foot, alone, in darkness, without them.

Lynne Wycherley

Watching the Tide on Inch Strand

We breathe salt light, the bright strand
stretched for four miles. Almost blinding.
Walkers dwindle, a scatter
of letters by an unknown hand.

Beachcombers. Dogs. Lovers curved in a single line
that runs from heart
to source to heart again,
their silhouettes inked against the shine

on love's horizon
where the infinite comes to us running
in long white waves
on a table of revelation.

Here we are destined to be small,
washed in the sea's wide roar
where light unpours
successively on light. Filling our shells.

Padraig Rooney

The Nuns at Poll an tSnámh

After thirty years holding their breath
they break the surface this morning,
Sisters Attracta, Concepta, Assumpta.
They're wearing flour bags gathered
by elastic at the top, unstitched below,
to shield themselves from prying eyes.
Three young nuns at *Poll an tSnámh*
undressing, fluent Irish on the wind,
the summer men landed on the moon.
Their habits, veils, coifs come off
until they're in their pelts under the bags
with *Odlums Flour* stencilled on them.
It's the only nuns' striptease we've seen,
or will ever see. They approach the edge
whiteskinned in their dark bathing suits.
They're going in, going under, disappearing
into the green water of the deep end.

Seán Lysaght

A Stone's Throw

Released to the summer sea, we played skimming stones.
Each small discus hit eight, nine, or maybe ten times
before it faltered. We threw in the direction

that the planes were headed, taking off from Shannon
with their privileged set returning to the States.
We knew our station then, and used fragments of slate

or other well-shaped bits of stone for our scansion.
If you angled well on a calm stretch of water
you could extend the count to the syllables in

the British Overseas Airways Corporation,
that alexandrine along the length of the plane
we waved to the day Paddy went back to Boston.

He threaded the first path my stones were longing for
to America, to see myself checking in
with words to make the stone take off as metaphor.

Gerard Donovan

Steps to Possession

Stripped to the waist under noon sun,
I broke the skin of ocean
surging in the shallows
like a child at my feet.
My ankles lifted easily
from such feeble hands,
and I entered easily.

Ten steps later, the waves reached belly high,
cool and muscular,
gripping my hips like a dancer leading
with her fingertips, slowing me with certain grace,
kneading my back with pulsating arms,
my eyes wrapped in her green dress.

Lighter, I lifted with each wave
until water cradled my neck.
I swayed to that breathing clasp,
embraced in close dance,
counting the steps to your heart.

Tom MacIntyre

Menage-à-Trois na Maidne

Tá mo leannán sí, le haiteas,
ag muirniú mo leannáin luí
(fíoradh mo thairngreacht, fíoradh í),
anois ag súpláil ar a barraicíní,
anois — tá an páipéar balla teilgthe
ag luisniú le teann dúile . . .

Tá mo leannán sí — buíochas
le Dia is na Máithreacha —
lem shuirí, a súile lán d'anghrá,
a hanáil aibí, a leasracha
leabhaire ag leá na gcompás —
níl aon chompás ach iad . . .

Tá mise mé féin — duine ar a sheal —
ag muirniú mo leannáin luí,
ag déanamh máine lena táithín,
a poll slogaide naofa ag teacht i radharc—
'Níos deireanaí', adeir sí, ag brú
méanfaí fúithi, 'Níl fonn orm anois . . .'
Is tá sí i sorm suain.

My *leannán sí* (without restraint)/ fondles my *leannán luí* —/ I saw this coming — now it's/ the nipple horzey-dervishes,/ next — the wall-paper blushes. . .// My *leannán sí* — thanks/ be to Christ and The Great Mothers/ turns her attention to me,/ breath, tongue, inflammatory thighs/ melt the compass, there is/ no compass but she. . .// Our turn. I beam attention/ on my *leannán luí,*/ pianissimo her pubic fuzz,/ summon that capricious/ pussy to — 'Later, *a chroí,*/ she drives back a yawn,/ 'Later, okay?' And. She sleeps.

Leannán sí: fairy, phantom lover
Leannán Luí: concubine, paramour
Foclóir: Niall Ó Domhnaill

Rita Ann Higgins

They never wear Coats

They start early on Friday night
in the girlfriends house.
They pour into the new clothes
from Fenwicks
or the bargain rail.

These tubes on legs
high heels on stilts
will paint the town red.
A swig for you
A swig for me
'that looks lovely on ya hinny,
I'd nearly do ya meself'

With perfect Revlon faces
they hit Newcastle
linking each other
six or seven across.
Close enough to trade
secret for Geordie secret.

When eleven comes
they fall from Grace
onto the nite club queue
Carol as always has to pee,
'Have ya had a good look like,
I'll shove yer face in it for ya'?

More laughter, eye contact is made
the bonding started long before this
in another pub in The Big Mart.
A glance that lingered longer than a second
is at least the promise of a blow job.

They look like models
same shaky walk

same knicker jaw-line
they never wear coats.

The bouncers can look all they like
through their gable end shoulders.
They have close shaves
they have no necks
they list on the soles of their feet,
a practiced technique.
They say one of them done it for a week
without blinking.
The money raised went to
the battered bouncers ball.

In the lane
near Tyneside Cinema
earlier glances are being metamorphosed.
Shadows fumble, they nearly fall
with heart stopping ticks of lust.

They know the words of all the songs
they sing them all day in the workplace
'I try to say goodbye and I choke
I try to walk away and I stumble'
this night they sing louder
helped by vodka and gin.

Again they link their precious friends
they are ready for Geordie
no need to beat around the bush
they speak his language.

'I'll shag him the nite
and he won't know what hit him
big Geordie fuck.'

Rita Ann Higgins

Our Brother the Pope
For Fr. Pat O'Brien
Sorrow is better than laughter,
for by a sad countenance the heart is made better.
— *Ecclesiastes*

Few people know this
but Pope John the 23rd
was a member of our family
his real name was Pope John the 23rd Higgins.

He lived with us in Ballbrit
I can't say he had his own room
but he didn't need it
he had his own house
our house.

He was there
when our father
brought home the mackerel
when Yahweh Curran
whistled his way
round the twelve cottages.

He was there when we
painted the house
for the races
and when we
got the new range
Stanley the 9th.

When he died
nothing was the same,
The mackerel began to stink
Yahweh Curran didn't whistle
for a solid month
the picture show in Silk's Shed
was just a runaway wagon

with three wheels
Our mother cried and cried.
Saint Jude and Saint Agnes
let her down big time
as for poor Philomena,
she couldn't conjure up
a minor miracle if her life depended on it
she was gone by the board.

The neighbours who were well clued in
queued up round the cottages
to offer their condolence
they were soaking in grief.

We're sorry about the mackerel
they said one after the other
holding their noses.
Our mother cried louder.

John McAuliffe

After Goethe's Fifth Roman Elegy

The presence of the past almost suffocates.
Walking, the streets are like a graveyard.
I turn to my books to make some sense
Of its proximities, spending the days
Reading in the garden at my leisure.

But at night I am called to endeavours
That are two-sided, only half mine,
And twice more pleasure — it is then
That I am truly escaped. I step
Over the blue pool of our clothes on the floor
And gaze at the white breast down the hip
Where I'm now guiding my hand.

Though my beloved keeps me from the dawn
She makes up for those hours in the dark.
But we are not only kissing, we talk
Wisely, and if she sleeps, breathing steadily
(She shakes for one instant first), I gently
Count out a pentameter on her warm back.

Then, a fire's lit in my heart — the old gods
Look on us as they've looked for millennia
At the clear margin of disaster and confusion.

Gerry Murphy

Ode 32
after Catullus

Give me a call this afternoon
if you have nothing else on,
especially clothes.
We could make love
into the evening and beyond.
Leave the back door off the latch,
tie up that snarling mastiff,
don't change your mind
and go shopping.
Get ready in your room
to come at least nine times
in quick succession,
just for starters.
In fact, I can come over right now.
I'm just lounging on the sofa,
stroking myself,
wondering what to do next
with this twitching erection.

Kate Dempsey

Running out

I mean to say
'Why is it so difficult?'
Doesn't he see it?
The empty roll.
The replacement standing fatly
I mean to say
'Just spring it out and change it.
Is it so hard?'
My grandmother told me
'Men don't see dirt.'
Men don't see.
I mean to say
'Just change it, why can't you?'
I say
'Just change.'

Michael Cronin

Cheating Death

Weather Permitting, **Dennis O'Driscoll**, Anvil, 1999, £7.95.

John Millington Synge noted a familiar human complaint when returning to his cottage one evening he thought, 'in what a little while I would be in my grave with the whole world lost to me.' The littleness of a while is a matter of opinion. Fear of death torments the young as much as its certainty unnerves the old. It is one of poetry's most enduring allies and also one of its most unreliable. The temptation of platitudinous solemnity is great when Love, Death, Beauty, Truth are put through their paces in Allegories of Life. The particular achievement of Dennis O'Driscoll in his excellent, new collection is to cheat Death not of its human inevitability but of its poetic banality.

The title of the second section of the collection, 'Churchyard View: The New Estate' parodies the purple prose of the colour supplement realtors, ruin and tack rehabilitated by the hyberbole of restaurant menus. The verses are a dark reminder of the brittleness of worlds built on the utopian expectations of DIY breviaries:

> On their side, inviolable silence
> On ours, hammering, pounding,
> sawing, clawing out foundations
> with the frenzy of someone buried alive.

The meshing of the physical realities of death, the homes of the dead with the real estate of the living is realised in a series of intricate shifts of metaphor, image and idea, that bring the living and the dead into sharp, uncomfortable focus. Graveyards are also of course comedy cellars, and Máirtín Ó Cadhain in a suburban moment would have relished the lines:

> Who had a crush on the girl
> six headstones away.
> Who couldn't muster
> the courage.
> Who wouldn't make
> the first move.

In other poems in the first section, 'Either', 'In Memory of Alois Alzheimer', 'The Victim', 'Interim Reports', 'Deadlines', 'Towards a Cesare Pavese Title', the puzzling randomness of death is teased over, homely metaphors of domestic ordinariness pounced on by the sudden finality of disappearance and the awkward sick-room preludes. The poems are affecting and forceful but avoid the maudlin muddle of lament or the wintry joylessness of doomsmen. The 'dream-time before work' ('Either') is the music of our aliveness, not the threadbare worthlessness of our lives.

If death sees off loved ones, it welcomes in memory. In the third section, 'Family Album' is a long trawl through childhood and O'Driscoll excels in sharp, spare images that not only bring forth a past but call it endlessly into question:

> No work. No school.
> Sunday, January 20th 1963.
> Wary cars are testing
> fresh clots of snow.
> Crinkled seals of ice
> unbroken on puddles,
> rain-barrel frozen tight,
> what might our outlook hold
> when the icicle sword
> guarding the bay window
> corrodes and we gradually
> drift apart?

Parents are there in the 'Album', and the Church but what is most apparent is the profoundly sensuous engagement of the poet with the past picked over through words. A father's shaved chin, bread vans, hayfields, oranges ('gaudy leatherette of skin'), all are sensed through the almost tactile reach of the language. There is affection in remembrance, not the inconsolable keen for what no longer is but an oblique tribute to the unproclaimed kindness of parents who lived for whatever moments came and did not fuss over posterity. The detail of memory is also present in the striking attentiveness to objects, whether it is the peach in 'End of the Peach Season' or a snail in 'Snail's Pace'. A pictorial translation might be Flemish still life, where images are more than descriptions but representation as thought, a mind brooding on particulars:

> I look down on the snail as on a container ship
> seen from a plane, its slow pace an illusion
> caused by distance, filigree silver wash a ruff
> of sea spray.
>
> — 'Snail's Pace'

The contemporary satire which brought much attention to 'Quality Time' (particularly for 'The Bottom Line') is largely absent from this collection. 'Celtic Tiger' is one of the weaker poems in *Weather Permitting*, tending towards a catalogue of Irish consumerist giddiness but failing to leave the flatlands of sardonic statement. 'Delegates' is tighter, more elaborate with a genuine echo of emptiness ghosting the endless displacements of the corporate and institutional elites of our age. The humour is more playful in 'To a Love Poet', where the fortysomething love poet no longer 'a meaningful contender in the passion stakes' takes the dictionary into his arms and sets off for the Cythera of his lexical imagining, freighted with adjective, 'young and eligible for love again'.

O'Driscoll is a magnificently literate poet. Holub, Dsida, Klima, Mackay Brown, Leopardi are the visible traces of wide reading and attentive generosity to the work of others, a generosity that is no prisoner to geography or language. But he is above all, a distinctive and important voice in poetry, in Ireland and elsewhere, and *Weather Permitting* is a high-point of his achievement.

Stuart Lane
Ancient Earthworks

Ancient earthworks —
A raven echoes vanished
war cries.

Patrick Gerard Burke
Break TIme

break time —
a black coffee
and three aspirin snack

Jessica ní Chuaig
Imprints

barefoot woman flees
    nailed saxon boots
        across wet plaster

Bob Slaymaker
Disclaimer

No animals or plants
were harmed in the making
of this product.

Only people.

Mark Granier
Approaching Dun Aengus

Wave-thunder, the whole
island a tall house — downstairs
the sea's at the door.

Iggy McGovern

Museless

The sullen page
will not engage
with the thin pen;
no prayer or Zen
mantra divine
a single line
nor scan of ceiling
stir up feeling
nor cups of tea
breed verity,
just the curse
of being worse
than (m)useless?

Anatoly Kudryavitsky

Poet and Poverty

No one needs a poet

Somebody
sometimes
needs his verse
and buys it
dirt-cheap

Gabriel Rosenstock

Broighill sna Dugaí

Broighill sna dugaí
A sciatháin ar leathadh acu —
Dubhchéasadh

Cormorants in dockland/ Wings outstretched —/ Dark crucifixions.

Adam Rudden

Bury the Coffins

In the oven
I kept the past warm for you
But its tenderness has long dried.

Clair Dillon

If Sympathy is. . .

If sympathy is
Walking in another's shoes,
Then isn't compassion
Offering them your slippers?

Margaret Toppin

In my Veggie Box

In my veggie box
a pink sprouting potato
green stalked drills nudge.

John O'Donnell

Where A Poem Comes From

The roof that I fell off when I was ten
was at the back of an abandoned house
I'd been warned against, although

the thrill of loitering there
deliciously illicit after school
soon wore thin, a drama become casual

until the fall. What made me lose
my footing I don't know; carelessness,
day-dreaming or perhaps

pure chance shaping the drop
that left me on the ground
and roaring, pointing to my shin

at where the rusted hidden spike
had entered in. My eyes filled with
the bloom and ooze of blood at first

but it was the later pain that mattered
more, a deep dull throb that seemed to be
just *there*, under bedclothes or school trousers,

the new skin forming and reforming as I
kept giving in to the urge to pick at it
again, with finger-nail or pencil-point,

hoping for the cruel vivid slash
so many t.v. baddies wore, but ending up
instead, I don't remember when,

with a pale dent the shape
of a small flying fish which made
my class-mates smile. The house

is gone, lines of whitewash
rolled on tarmac, space to park
a hundred cars. And I still have the scar.

Jonathan Enfield

After the Workshop

This poem is looking for a job.
Its abstractions, you see, aren't concrete,
its sincerity is a smidge too sincere, and
what's worse, it's owned by its own conceit.

This poem seeks honest employment
as it lacks strange detail and metaphor.
It neither embraces its limitations,
nor bleeds a drop for the suffering poor.

This poem simply wishes to be of use:
it will work for food or gather sticks;
it will management-consult, de-bug, de-brief,
or stand slattern in alleys and turn tricks.

It has its defects, and we all know 'em
in short, it doesn't quite work as a poem.

Christine Broe

No Poem

The pencil squiggles
let it twist
the line of words that come
come only from the wrist,

eight bones
the westerly most
resting on the page
as I face the window.

White space.
If I were a snail
my silvery afterthoughts
at least would leave a trail
to shine
in the absence of a poem.

White page,
product of some tree
sacrificed, bleached,
set out upon a table
for pulp fiction.

In a state of too much mind
where do I find

white space

where words will settle,
where feeling and image will copulate,
cause a pregnant echo
in their wake.

I am not the vessel for such gift
today,
I will put the full stop here   .

Dennis O'Driscoll

Enveloped in Poetry

If I belong anywhere, it is among a school of poets about which surprisingly few doctoral theses have been written: The Back of the Envelope School. Members of this school are too busy to engage in literary intrigue and too stubbornly independent to endorse any particular style. To enrol in the school, you must draft your poems on the hoof because you do not enjoy the luxury of a fixed writing regime. Poets who earn a living in busy non-literary occupations are the archetypal Envelopers; my own membership arises from a job which keeps me out of the house and otherwise occupied for nearly twelve hours a day.

On the hotel bedroom desk at which — away from home on business — I jot down these remarks, there is an array of bonded notepaper bearing the words '*In Residence*' under the hotel name. Envelope poets may be literally 'in residence' in an organisation, company or even hotel, but they are never 'poets in residence'. Some wrong turning has left them pursuing ways of life which are entirely unconnected with poetry. They seldom, if ever, teach, preach, or profess it. Their patrons include Wallace Stevens, who would pause in the middle of dictating insurance letters and scribble down a phrase. Or his fellow-American, Eleanor Ross Taylor who remarked without bitterness, 'I would write just occasionally, just the poem that demanded it. . . I did keep the house scrubbed and waxed and that sort of thing.' Or, indeed, Philip Larkin who defined work as something you do in order to have spare time.

Back of the Envelopers are unlikely to be found in artists' colonies or in writers' workshops because their imaginative antennae would jam with self-consciousness at the very thought of being where one is *expected* to write. They are capable of producing poetry only on a surreptitious basis, when no one else is looking — ideally, when colleagues and neighbours don't remotely suspect them of association with so rarefied an activity.

99% inspiration and 1% perspiration is Envelopers' formula for a poem. It is not that they don't fully appreciate the need for the hard labour of revision — these are people, after all, who (albeit in other contexts) are well used to bringing ideas to frution. But re-vision is in essence an attempt to align each successive draft more closely with the vision which seared and soared through the imagination in the first place. The cryptic phrases which they jotted down between a staff appraisal and a client briefing are the chips of rosetta, the scraps of papyrus that speak of an elsewhere and an otherwise. For people driven to distraction by constant demands on their time, consolation lies in the fact that the essential work is already complete when those spontaneous scribblings light upon the back of an envelope or on a sheet of hotel paper. The rest — thought it may take week, months, years — is a mere tidying up afterwards.

Notes on Contributors

Chris Agee has published two collections, *In the New Hampshire Woods* (1992) and *The Sierra de Zacatecas* (1995). His third collection, *First Light*, is forthcoming.

Gary Allen was born and lives in Co. Antrim. He has been published widely in journals including *Acumen, Force 10, H.U., London Magazine,* and *Stand*. Lapwing published his pamphlet 'Mending Churches'.

Manny Blacksher is a graduate student in English studies at Trinity. His work has previously appeared in *Poetry Ireland Review* and he has upcoming work in *The Cúirt Journal, The Burning Bush* and *Books Ireland*.

Denise Blake lives in Letterkenny. She is a member of the Errigal Writers. The group recently published a collection of their poetry, *Beyond the Rubicon*.

Eva Bourke is originally from Germany. She has published three collections of poetry and has also translated Irish poetry into German. Her most recent collection is *Dinner with Gandolpho*.

Deirdre Brennan: trí leabhair filíochta dá cuid foilsithe as Coiscéim: *I Reilig na mBan Rialta, Scothanna Geala, Thar Cholbha na Mara*.

Fiona Brennan won the Scottish International Poetry Competition 2000, the Trewithen International Poetry Prize 1998 and was shortlisted for the OKI Literary Awards 1998. She has been published widely in Irish and English.

Christine Broe has been widely published in journals. She has taken part in the Poetry Ireland Introductions Series and was placed second in the Dublin Literary Festival Poetry Slam.

Patricia Burke Brogan's collection of poems and etchings *Above the Waves' Calligraphy* was published by Salmon 1994. Her stage play *Eclipsed* won an Edinburgh Fringe first and the USA Moss Hart Theatre Award 1994.

Patrick Gerard Burke is a former A.F.R.T.S. broadcaster and journalist. He currently works in the Department of Government, U.C.C.

Paddy Bushe lives in Kerry. His fourth collection is forthcoming from Dedalus.

Eileen Casey was twice winner of the George Moore Medallion, winner of the South Tipperary Literary Festival, the A.I.B./Western People and Poetry on the Wall Competition.

Harry Clifton was born in Dublin and lives in Paris. His second collection of poems, *Night Train Through the Brenner*, was published in 1994 by Gallery Press. A third collection is forthcoming.

Colette Connor's poems have appeared in *Poetry Ireland Review, H.U., Books Ireland, Cúirt, The Stinging Fly* etc. She has been shortlisted for the Hennessy Award.

Michael Cronin is head of Applied Languages at D.C.U. He is the author of

Translating Ireland, and more recently, *Across the Lines: Travel, Language and Translation* by Cork Univeristy Press, 2000.

Tony Curtis has published two collections with Beaver Row Press. His most recent collection is *This Far North* by Dedalus.

Máire de Búrca is a native of Sligo and is currently studying for an MA degree in Irish at National University of Ireland, Galway. She has been Irish language editor of *Ropes*.

Greg Delanty's collections include *Cast in the Fire* (1986) and *Southward* (1992). He received the Patrick Kavanagh Award in 1983 and The Allan Dowling Poetry Fellowship in 1986.

Kate Dempsey lives in Maynooth and is currently working on her first novel.

Louis de Paor's most recent collection is *Corach agus Dánta Eile* (Coiscéim), published bilingually in Australia as *Cork and Other Poems* (Black Pepper). He is recipient of the O'Shaughnessy Award 2000.

Greg Delanty's most recent book is *The Hellbox* (O.U.P.). His next collection *Leper's Way* is due from Carcanet in 2001.

Clair Dillon lives in Vancouver.

Moyra Donaldson's first collection *Snakeskin Stilettos* was published by Lagan Press in 1998. Her second, *Words in the Mirror* is forthcoming.

Gerard Donovan has been published in *The Irish Times*, *Poetry Ireland Review*, *Stand*, and others. His collection, *The Lighthouse* is due from Salmon this year.

Jonathan Enfield studies south of the Liffey, gets his mail north of it and is working on a novel and a book of poems.

Tom French's poems have appeared in *Cyphers, H.U., Metre, Poetry Ireland Review, Shenandoah, Stand, Thumbscrew* and elsewhere. He lives in Dublin.

Mark Granier's poems have appeared in *Poetry Ireland Review, The Irish Times, T.L.S.* and elsewhere. His first collection is forthcoming from Salmon.

James Gross was raised on the shores of Lake Michigan. He is a poet, guitar player, and songwriter. He has been published in six states, Canada and Ireland.

Maurice Harmon is a previous contributor to *Poetry Ireland Review*. His collection *The Last Regatta*, will appear from Salmon this summer.

Rita Ann Higgins' forthcoming collection is due from Bloodaxe in 2001. Her collection *Sunnyside Plucked* was a Poetry Book Society Recommendation.

Fred Johnston lives in Galway and has published seven collections of poetry, a novel and a collection of short stories. He won a Hennessy Prize and won the *Sunday Independent* Prose and Poetry Awards twice.

Rita Kelly was born in Galway. She has published three collections and is currently Writer in Residence in Cavan. Her forthcoming collection is due in autum from Arlen House.

Kevin Kiely is New Writing Editor of *Books Ireland*. His poems have appeared in *Anvil, Criterion, The Belle, Edinburgh Review, Poetry Ireland Review, Cyphers, Incognito* and others.

John Knowles has been previously published in *Poetry Ireland Review*, the 1999 *Tabla Book of New Verse, H.U., Irish News* and *Oxford Poetry*.

Anatoly Kudryavitsky's seven books of poetry include *The Field of Eternal Stories* (1996) and *Grafitti* (1998), both by Third Wave Publishing. His poems have been translated into English, French, German, Spanish, Hebrew and Chinese.

Stuart Lane is a poet and linguist living in Co. Kildare. He is currently working on his second book, a collection of haiku entitled *Ripples in a Dark Pool*.

Eamonn Lynskey's poetry has appeared widely in publications such as *Poetry Ireland Review, Cyphers* and *The Stinging Fly*. His first collection, *Dispatches and Recollections* was published by Lapwing in 1998.

Seán Lysaght has published three collections, *Noah's Irish Ark* (Dedalus, 1989), *The Clare Island Survey* (Gallery, 1991), and *Scarecrow* (Gallery, 1998).

Pádraig Mac Fhearghusa: idir fhilíocht agus stair scríofa aige. Leabhar ar an tsíocanailís, *Toraíocht an Mhísonais*, i gcló aige. Eagarthóir ar an míosachán liteartha Feasta é. Bhuaigh a chnuasach *Mearcair* príomhdhuais fhilíocht an Oireachtais i 1996.

John McAuliffe has published poems in *The Irish Times, The Sunday Tribune, Ropes* and other journals. He recently received the RTE Poet of the Future Award.

Cecilia McGovern's poems have been published in the *Sunday Tribune, Poetry Ireland Review, Anthology Womens' Day* 1991, 1993, 1995, 1993. She was the prizewinner of the Dun Laoghaire Arts Festival 1991.

Iggy McGovern received the Hennessy Award for poetry in 1996.

Tom McFadden lives in Texas. His work has been widely published in journals such as *Poetry Ireland Review, Poet's Voice, Poetry New York, Seattle Review, Pittsburgh Quarterly* and others.

Tom MacIntyre is a member of Aosdána. His most recent collection, *Stories of the Wandering Moon*, is published by Lilliput Press.

Liz McSkeane was born in Glasgow and lives in Dublin. She won the Emerging Poetry Section of the Hennessy New Irish Writing Awards 1999 and was the overall winner of the New Irish Writer of the Year Award.

Patrick Moran's poems have appeared in *Cyphers, The Honest Ulsterman, Force 10, Poetry Ireland Review, The Cúirt Journal*, and *New Irish Writing*. He was shortlisted for the Hennessy/*Sunday Tribune* Award and *The Irish Times*.

Art Murphy's poems have appeared in *Poetry Ireland Review, Chapman* (Edinburgh), *The New Welsh Review, Agenda* and *Magma* (London), *Books Ireland, The Irish News* and *H.U.*.

Gerry Murphy was born and lives in Cork. His most recent collections include *The Empty Quarter* (Dedalus, 19950 and *Real de la Plata and All That* (Dedalus, 1993).

Nuala Ní Chonchúir's poetry has been published in *The Cúirt Journal, Books Ireland* and elswhere. She is a founder member of Garters, a women' writing group in Galway.

Jessica Ní Chuaig has a Cambridge doctorate in medieval English. She teacher and researches in London and is writing poetry, plays and a screenplay.

Bríd Ní Mhóráin: Cónaí uirthi i gCorca Dhuibhne. Tá a lán duaiseanna Oireachtais buaite aici. Foilsíodh dánta léi in *Innti, Feasta, Comhar, An tUltach, Samhlaíocht Aniar,* agus is minic í ag léamh ag Féilte agus ar an Raidió.

D. Nurkse received the 1998 Bess Hokin Prize for Poetry (Chicago). Forthcoming works include *Leaving Xaia* and *The Rules of Paradise* (both from Four Way Books) and poems in *The Paris Review* and *The New Yorker*.

Jean O'Brien is a founding member of Dublin Writers' Workshop. Her collection *The Shadow Keeper* was published by Salmon in 1997.

Bernard O'Donoghue is a Whitbread prizewinning poet. His most recent collection of poems, *Here Nor There*, which was published by Chatto and Windus in 1999. He now lives in England and lectures at Oxford.

Dennis O'Driscoll's fifth collection, *Weather Permitting,* is a Poetry Book Society Recommendation.

John O'Donnell has been widely published. He won the Hennessy/ *Sunday Tribune* Award in 1998. He also won the Listowel Prize for Poetry in the same year.

Sheila O'Hagan's collections include *The Peacock's Eye* and *The Troubled House*. She holds the Patrick Kavanagh, the Hennessy/ *Sunday Tribune* and the Strokestown Awards for poetry.

Una O'Higgins O'Malley has been published by the Australian-Irish network. She is currently working on a collection of poems *Twentieth Century Revisited* and on her memoirs *From Pardon and Protest.*

Pádraig ó Snodaigh: stairí, file agus foilsitheoir ó Cheatharlach. Cnuasach filíochta dá chuid *Ó Pharnell go Queenie,* aistrithe ag Mícheál Ó Fionnán, le foilsiú go luath ag Lapwing. Dán fada leis foilsithe ag Mobydick i bhfaienza na hIodáile.

Derry O'Sullivan won the Oireachtas Seán Ó Riordán Prize in 1987. His collections *Cá bhfuil do Iudas* and *Cá bhfuil Tiarna Talun L'Univers* are published by Coiscéim. His most recents collection, *En Mals de Fleurs* is published in French.

Paul Perry's first collection *The Drowning of the Saints* is forthcoming from Salmon. He won the Hennessy New Irish Writer of the Year Award in 1998.

Padraig Rooney has won Patrick Kavanagh Award for his collection *In the Bonsai*

Garden. His poems have appeared in various journals and *Scanning the Century:* The *Penguin Book of Twentieth Century in Poetry*.

Gabriel Rosenstock lives in Dublin. His most recent works include *Bróg Kruschev agus Scéalta Eile*, and the children's picture book *An Rógaire agus a Scáil*.

Adam Rudden is a student at Fingal Community College, Swords. His poem 'Sandman's Storms' has been chosen by the International Library of Poetry for publication.

Peter Sirr is editor of *Graph* and director of the Irish Writers Centre. He has published four collections with Gallery Press and his fifth, *Bring Everything*, is forthcoming.

Bob Slaymaker lives in New York. His poems have appeared in many journals including *New York Quarterly, Press, Writers Forum, Callaloo* and others.

Dawn Sullivan has had work broadcast on RTE. In 1998 she came joint second in the Salisbury Festival Competition. She has been published in *Camden* and *Poetry Now*.

Ronald Tamplin's poems have appeared widely. Awards include The Eugene Lee-Hamilton Prize, The City of Winchester John Keats Bi-Centennial Prize and a Commendation in the 1998 National Poetry Competition.

Margaret Toppin's first collection is *African Violets*. She has been a prizewinner in the Syllables, Cúirt, Riposte, Jonathan Swift, South Tipperary, Clough and Scottish International Poetry Competitions.

Mary Wickham's collection, *In the Water Was the Fire*, is published by Spectrum. She lives and teachers in Australia.

Merryn Williams' first collection *The Sun's Yellow Eye* won the Rosemary Arthur Award. Her second collection is forthcoming from Rockingham. She is translator of the *Selected Poems of Federico Garcia Lorca* (Bloodaxe).

Howard Wright's first collection *Usquebaugh* was published by Redbeck in 1997. He won The Kilkenny Short Story Prize 1997 and The Kilkenny Poetry Prize 1998. He also received the Martin Healy Short Story Award.

Lynne Wycherley lives in England. Her collection *Cracks in the Ice* is published by Acumen and she has won the Blue Nose Poet of the Year Competition.

Books Received

Mention here does not preclude a review in a future issue.

Cork Literary Review, Vol. VI, 1999/2000.
Atlanta Review, Autumn/ Winter, 1999.
Carole Satyamurti, *Love and Variations*, Bloodaxe.
Ed. by Jeff Adams, *Don Marquis: Archyology ii*, Bloodaxe.
Redlamp, Issue 6, Spring/ Summer.
Chris Arthurs, *Irish Nocturnes*, Davies Group Publishers.
Noel Keaveney, *A Long Scattering*, Bradshaw Books.
Basil Bunting, *Complete Poems*, Bloodaxe.
Ed. by Tim Kendall, *Thumbscrew 15*.
Ed. by Chris Agee, *Scar on the Stone*, Bloodaxe.
Dolores Stewart, *In Out of the Rain*, Dedalus.
Ed. by David Pike, *Pulsar*, Edition 1/00 (21).
Ed. by Michael Koch, *Epoch*, Vol. 48, No. 3.
Basil Griffiths, Anni WiIlton-Jones, Jeff Rees, Clair Syder, *This is . . . Salem*, Stonebridge.
Jeff Rees, *Dandelion Time*, Stonebridge.
Mike Byrne, *Storm of Words*, Stonebridge.
Catherine Fisher, *Altered States*, Seren.
Madison Morrison, *A Warfilm is Peacefilm*, Tharami Selvi Pathippagam.
Ed. by David Hamilton and Mary Hussmann, *The Iowa Review*, Vol. 23, No. 3.
Ed. by W.J. Cormack, *Ferocious Humanism: an Anthology of Irish Poetry from Before Swift and After*, Dent.
Ed. Thomas Dillon Redshaw, *New Hibernia Review/ Iris Éireannach Nua*, Vol. 3, No. 4.
Matthew Sweeney, *A Smell of Fish*, Cape Poetry.
Lévres Baines 30.
Le Gearóid MacLochlainn, *Sa Chathair: New Songs for Children and Learners in Gaelic* (Cassette), Outlet.
Basil Bunting, *Briggflatts and Other Poems* (Cassette), Bloodaxe.
Ed. by Leland Bardwell, Eiléan ní Chuilleanáin, Pearse Hutchinson, Macdara Woods, *Cyphers* 47.
S.P. Zitner, *The Asparagus Feast*, McGill-Queens University Press.
David O'Meara, *Storm Still*, McGill-Queens University Press.
Ed. by Niall McGrath, *The Black Mountain Review*, Issue 2, January 2000.
Lewis Regan, *Regan*, The Milestone L Press.
Michael Longley, *The Weather in Japan*, Cape Poetry.
Ed. by Tom Clyde, *H.U.*, Issue 108, Winter '99/ '00.
Ed. by Robin Hemley, *Bellingham Review*, Vol. XXII, No. 2.
Ed. by Nancy J. Curtin and Vera Kreilkamp, *Éire/Ireland*, Summer 1999.
Mimi Khalvati, *Selected Poems*, Carcanet.
Sujata Bhatt, *Augatora*, Carcanet.

Jamie McKendrick, *Sky Nails: Poems 1979-1997*, Faber and Faber.
Stephen Dobyns, *Pallbearers Envying The One Who Rides*, Bloodaxe.
Douglas Oliver, *A Salvo for Africa*, Bloodaxe.
Owen Sheers, *The Blue Book*, Seren.
Frances Williams, *Wild Blue*, Seren.
Ed. by Joy Hendry, *Chapman 95*.
Ed. by Deborah Tall, *The Seneca Review*, Vol. 30, No. 1, Spring 2000.
Tony Curtis, *This Far North*, Dedalus.
Mary Guckian, *Perfume of the Soil*, Swan Press.
Ed. by Greg McCartney, *The Chancer*, Issue 4.
Ed. by Michael Bishop, Salah Stétié: *Cold Water Shielded*, Bloodaxe Contemporary French Poets 10, Bloodaxe.
Neville Keery, *Turnings*, Hinds.
Polly Clark, *Kiss*, Bloodaxe.
Roddy Lumsden, *The Book of Love*, Bloodaxe.
Fleur Adcock, *Poems 1960-2000*, Bloodaxe.
Alison Brackenbury, *After Beethoven*, Carcanet.
Chris Greenhalgh, *Of Love, Death and the Sea-Squirt*, Bloodaxe.
Julie O'Callaghan, *No Can Do*, Bloodaxe.
Elaine Feinstein, *Gold*, Carcanet.
John Ennis, *Tráithníní*, Dedalus.
Jean Valentine, *The Cradle of the Real Life*, Wesleyan University Press.
John A. Kessler, *Reflections in Poetry*, Buy Books.
Ed. Louis De Paor, Michael Davitt, *The Oomph of Quicksilver*, Cork University Press.
D. Nurkse, *Leaving Xaia*, Four Way Books.
Douglas Dunn, *The Donkey's Ears*, Faber and Faber.
Alan Jenkins, *The Drift*, Chatto and Windus.
Michael Kelly, *Light Disorderly*, Red Beck Press.
Keith Douglas, *The Complete Poems*, Faber and Faber.
Ian McElhinney, *The Green Shoot: A Life of John Hewitt*, Lagan Press
Ed. by Damian Smyth, *John Hewitt: Two Plays*, Lagan Press.
Hugh Maxton, *Gubu Roi*, Lagan Press.
Sam Gardiner, *Protestant Windows*, Lagan Press.
Ed. by Christopher Howell, *Willow Springs*, No. 45, January 2000.
Ed. Ted Sheehy, *Film Ireland 75*, April/ May 2000.
Noel Monahan, *Curse of the Birds*, Salmon.
William Larkin, *Millennium Poem from the Beyond*, Dillons Publishing.
William Larkin, *Eternity and Philip Larkin*, Dillon Publishing.
Ed. by P.J. Mathews, *New Voices in Irish Criticism*, Four Courts Press.
Ed. by Michael Mackmin, *The Rialto*, No. 45, Spring 2000.
Carlo Gébler, *Dance of Death*, Parts I and II, adapted from Strindberg's play cycle.
Pól Ó Muirí, *Is Mise Ísméal*, Lagan Press.

Previous Editors of Poetry Ireland Review

John Jordan 1-8	Spring 1981 - Autumn 1983
Thomas McCarthy 9-12	Winter 1983 - Winter 1984
Conleth Ellis & Rita E. Kelly 13	Spring 1985
Terence Brown 14-17	Autumn 1985 - Autumn 1986
Ciarán Cosgrove 18/19	Spring 1987
Dennis O'Driscoll 20-21	Autumn 1987 - Spring 1988
John Ennis & Rory Brennan 22/23	Summer 1988
John Ennis 24-25	Winter 1988 - Spring 1989
Micheal O'Siadhail 26-29	Summer 1989 - Summer 1990
Máire Mhac an tSaoi 30-33	Autumn 1990 - Winter 1991
Peter Denman 34-37	Spring 1992 - Winter 1992
Pat Boran 38	Summer 1993
Seán Ó Cearnaigh 39	Autumn 1993
Pat Boran 40-42	Winter 1993 - Summer 1994
Chris Agee 43/44	Autumn/Winter 1994
Moya Cannon 45-48	Spring 1995 - Winter 1995
Liam Ó Muirthile 49	Spring 1996
Michael Longley 50	Summer 1996
Liam Ó Muirthile 51,52	Autumn 1996 - Spring 1997
Frank Ormsby 53-56	Summer 1997 - Spring 1998
Catherine Phil Mac Carthy 57-60	Summer 1998 - Spring 1999
Mark Roper	Summer 1999 - Spring 2000